e e cummings *i*

SIX NONLECTURES

harvard university press

cambridge, massachusetts

london, england

Library of Congress Catalog Card Number
53-10472
ISBN 0-674-44010-2

Typography by
BURTON L. STRATTON

PRINTED IN THE UNITED STATES OF AMERICA

For John Finley

i &

my parents

NONLECTURE ONE

Let me cordially warn you, at the opening of these socalled lectures, that I haven't the remotest intention of posing as a lecturer. Lecturing is presumably a form of teaching; and presumably a teacher is somebody who knows. I never did, and still don't, know. What has always fascinated me is not teaching, but learning; and I assure you that if the acceptance of a Charles Eliot Norton professorship hadn't rapidly entangled itself with the expectation of learning a very great deal, I should now be somewhere else. Let me also assure you that I feel extremely glad to be here; and that I heartily hope you won't feel extremely sorry.

Ever since many of you didn't exist I've been learning and relearning, as a writer and as a painter, the significance of those immemorial maxims "one man's meat is another man's poison" and "you can lead the mare to water but you can't make her drink." Now—as a nonlecturer—I am luckily confronted by that equally ancient, but far less austere, dictum "it's an ill wind which blows nobody good." For while a genuine lecturer must obey the rules of mental decency, and clothe his personal idiosyncrasies in collectively acceptable generalities, an authentic ignoramus remains quite indecently free to speak as he feels. This prospect cheers me, because I value freedom; and have never expected freedom to be anything less than indecent. The very fact that a burlesk addict of long standing (who has many times worshipped at the shrine of progressive corporeal revelation) finds himself on the verge of attempting an aesthetic striptease, strikes me as a quite remarkable manifestation of poetic justice; and reinforces my conviction that since I can't tell you what I know (or rather what I don't know) there's nothing to prevent me from trying to tell you who I am—which I'd deeply enjoy doing.

But who am I? Or rather—since my drawing and painting self concerns you not at all—who is my other self, the self of the prose and of the poetry? Here I perceive a serious problem; as well as an excellent chance to learn something. There'd be no problem, of course, if I subscribed to the hyperscientific doctrine that heredity is nothing because everything is environment; or if (having swallowed this supersleepingpill) I envisaged the future of socalled mankind as a permanent pastlessness, prenatally enveloping semiidentical supersubmorons in perpetual nonunhappiness. Rightly or wrongly, however, I prefer spiritual insomnia to psychic suicide. The hellless hell of compulsory heaven-on-earth emphatically isn't my pail of blueberries. By denying the past, which I respect, it negates the future—and I love the future. Consequently for me an autobiographical problem is an actuality.

Inspecting my autobiographical problem at close range, I see that it comprises two problems; united by a certain wholly mysterious moment which signifies selfdiscovery. Until this mysterious moment, I am only incidentally a writer: primarily I am the son of my parents and whatever is happening to him. After this moment, the question "who am I?" is answered by what I write—in other words, I become my writing; and my autobiography becomes the exploration of my stance as a writer. Two questions now make their appearance. The first—what constitutes this writing of mine?—can be readily answered: my writing consists of a pair of miscalled novels; a brace of plays, one in prose, the other in blank verse; nine books of poems; an indeterminate number of essays; an untitled volume of satire; and a ballet scenario. The second question—where, in all this material, do I find my stance as a writer most clearly expressed?—can be answered almost as readily: I find it expressed most clearly in the later miscalled novel, the two plays, perhaps twenty poems, and half a dozen of the essays. Very well; I shall build the second part of my autobiography around this prose and this poetry, allowing (wherever possible) the prose and the poetry to speak for themselves. But the first part of my autobiography presents a problem of another order

4

entirely. To solve that problem, I must create a longlost personage—my parents' son—and his vanished world. How can I do
this? I don't know; and because I don't know, I shall make the
attempt. Having made the attempt, I shall tackle my second
problem. If either attempt fails, I shall at least have tried.
And if both attempts succeed, I shall (by some miracle) have
achieved the impossible. For then—and only then—will you and
I behold an aesthetic selfportrait of one whole half of this and
no other indivisible ignoramus As Is.

Some, if not most, of the distinguished members of this enlight-
ened audience are now (I suspect) internally exclaiming "alas.
We come here expecting that a poet will lecture on poetry; and
the very first thing the socalled poet does is to tell us he hasn't
the slightest intention of doing so. Next, the socalled poet in-
dulges in a lot of pretty corny backtracking; all of which proves
exactly nothing, unless it's that as a draughtsman he doesn't
know his gluteus maximus from his olecranon. Finally (adding
injury to insult) the socalled poet graciously announces that we
may expect him to favor us with a description of his prepoetic
career, and then—as if this weren't bad enough—with a bevy
of largely prosaic tidbits which have occasionally escaped him
in the course of the last three decades: because only in this
manner can he possibly understand who he is today. Why in
the name of common sense doesn't the poet (socalled) read us
some poetry—any poetry; even his own—and tell us what he
thinks or doesn't think of it? Is the socalled poet a victim of
galloping egocentricity or is he just plain simpleminded?"

My immediate response to such a question would be: and why
not both? But supposing we partially bury the hatchet and
settle for egocentricity—who, if I may be so inconsiderate as to
ask, isn't egocentric? Half a century of time and several conti-
nents of space, in addition to a healthily developed curiosity,
haven't yet enabled me to locate a single peripherally situated

ego. Perhaps I somehow simply didn't meet the right people, and vice versa. At any rate, my slight acquaintance with senators pickpockets and scientists leads me to conclude that they are far from unselfcentred. So, I believe, are all honest educators. And so (I'm convinced) are streetcleaners deafmutes murderers mothers, mountainclimbers cannibals fairies, strong men beautiful women unborn babes international spies, ghostwriters bums business executives, out and out nuts cranks dopefiends policemen, altruists (above all) ambulancechasers obstetricians and liontamers. Not forgetting morticians—as undertakers (in this epoch of universal culture) prefer to denominate themselves. Or, as my friend the distinguished biographer M R Werner once subrosafully remarked, over several biscuit duboûchés "when you come right down to it, everybody's the whole boxoftricks to himself; whether she believes it or not."

Now let me make you a strictly egocentric proposition. Assuming that a socalled lecture lasts fifty minutes, I hereby solemnly swear to devote the last fifteen minutes of each and every lecture to nothing but poetry—and (what's more) poetry for which I am in no way whatever responsible. This will leave me only thirty-five minutes of any lecture to chatter unpoetically about myself; or (now and again) to read part of a poem— perhaps an entire poem—of my own. The unpoetical chattering will begin with my parents and proceed to their son, will touch upon selfdiscovery; and then (at nonlecture number four) will shift to an exploration of EECummings' stance as a writer. By contrast, the poetry readings will run clean through all six lectures; forming a strictly amateur anthology, or collection of poetry which for no reason or unreason I dearly love. In the course of my six halfhours of egocentricity I shall (among other deeds) discuss the difference between fact and truth, I shall describe professor Royce and the necktie crisis, I shall name professor Charles Eliot Norton's coachman, and I shall define sleep. If you ask "but why include trivialities?" my answer will

be: what are they? During my six fifteenminute poetry readings,
I shall only try to read poetry as well as I don't know how.
If you object "but why not criticize as well?" I shall quote very
briefly from a wonderful book, whose acquaintance I first made
through a wonderful friend named Hildegarde Watson—a book
whose English title is Letters To A Young Poet, and whose
author is the German poet Rainer Maria Rilke:

Works of art are of an infinite loneliness and with nothing to be so
little reached as with criticism. Only love can grasp and hold and
fairly judge them.

In my proud and humble opinion, those two sentences are
worth all the soi-disant criticism of the arts which has ever
existed or will ever exist. Disagree with them as much as you
like, but never forget them; for if you do, you will have forgotten the mystery which you have been, the mystery which
you shall be, and the mystery which you are—

so many selves(so many fiends and gods
each greedier than every)is a man
(so easily one in another hides;
yet man can,being all,escape from none)

so huge a tumult is the simplest wish:
so pitiless a massacre the hope
most innocent(so deep's the mind of flesh
and so awake what waking calls asleep)

so never is most lonely man alone
(his briefest breathing lives some planet's year,
his longest life's a heartbeat of some sun;
his least unmotion roams the youngest star)

—how should a fool that calls him "I" presume
to comprehend not numerable whom?

And thus we arrive at the parents of a longlost personage, who is these parents' child.

By way of describing my father, let me quote a letter and tell you a story. The letter was written by me to my good friend Paul Rosenfeld; who used it in an essay which graced the fifth number of that ambiguously entitled periodical The Harvard Wake:

I wot not how to answer your query about my father. He was a New Hampshire man, 6 foot 2, a crack shot & a famous fly-fisherman & a firstrate sailor (his sloop was named The Actress) & a woodsman who could find his way through forests primeval without a compass & a canoeist who'd stillpaddle you up to a deer without ruffling the surface of a pond & an ornithologist & taxidermist & (when he gave up hunting) an expert photographer (the best I've ever seen) & an actor who portrayed Julius Caesar in Sanders Theatre & a painter (both in oils & watercolours) & a better carpenter than any professional & an architect who designed his own houses before building them & (when he liked) a plumber who just for the fun of it installed all his own waterworks & (while at Harvard) a teacher with small use for professors—by whom (Royce, Lanman, Taussig, etc.) we were literally surrounded (but not defeated)—& later (at Doctor Hale's socalled South Congregational really Unitarian church) a preacher who announced, during the last war, that the Gott Mit Uns boys were in error since the only thing which mattered was for man to be on God's side (& one beautiful Sunday in Spring remarked from the pulpit that he couldn't understand why anyone had come to hear him on such a day) & horribly shocked his pewholders by crying "the Kingdom of Heaven is no spiritual roofgarden: it's inside you" & my father had the first telephone in Cambridge & (long before any Model T Ford) he piloted an Orient Buckboard with Friction Drive produced by the Waltham watch company & my father sent me to a certain public school because its principal was a gentle immense coalblack negress & when he became a diplomat (for World Peace) he gave me & my friends a tremendous party up in a tree at Sceaux Robinson & my father was a servant of the people who fought Boston's biggest & crookedest politician fiercely all day & a few evenings later sat down with him cheerfully at the Rotary Club & my father's voice was so magnificent that he was called on to impersonate God speaking from Beacon Hill (he was heard all over the common) & my father gave me Plato's metaphor of the cave with my mother's milk.

This, I feel, is an accurate sketch of Edward Cummings, Harvard '83—except as regards his neighbourliness. He certainly had "small use for professors" in general; but with the particular professors around him his relations were nearly always amicable and in certain cases affectionate. The neighbour whom my father unquestionably preferred was William James; and it's odd that I should have forgotten to mention so true a friend and so great a human being. Not only is it odd: it's ungrateful—since I may be said to owe my existence to professor James, who introduced my father to my mother.

Now for the story.

Thirty-five years ago, a soiled envelope with a French stamp on it arrived at 104 Irving Street, Cambridge. The envelope contained a carefully phrased scrawl; stating (among other things) that I was interned in a certain concentration camp, with a fine friend named Brown whom I'd met on the boat going to France—he, like myself, having volunteered as an ambulance driver with Messers Norton (not Charles Eliot) and Harjes. Immediately my father—than whom no father on this earth ever loved or ever will love his son more profoundly—cabled his friend Norton; but Mr Norton hadn't even missed us, and consequently could do less than nothing. Next, through a mere but loyal acquaintance, my father set the American army on our trail; forcefully stipulating that my friend and I must be rescued together. Many days passed. Suddenly the telephone rang—top brass demanding Reverend Edward Cummings. "Hello" my father said. "This is Major Soandso" an angry voice sputtered. "That friend of your son is no damned good. May even be a spy. Unpatriotic anyhow. He deserves what's coming

to him. Do you understand?" "I understand" said my deeply
patriotic father. "We won't touch Brown" the sputter continued
"so it's your son or nothing. And I guarantee that your son
alone will be out of that hellhole in five days—what do you say
about that?" "I say" replied my father "don't bother." And
he hung up.

Incidentally, the major bothered; and as a result, my friend
Slater Brown is also alive.

Let me only add that while my father was speaking with the
American army, my mother was standing beside him; for these
two wonderful human beings, my father and my mother, loved
each other more than themselves—

if there are any heavens my mother will(all by herself)have
one. It will not be a pansy heaven or
a fragile heaven of lilies-of-the-valley but
it will be a heaven of blackred roses

my father will be(deep like a rose
tall like a rose)

standing near my

(swaying over her
silent)
with eyes which are really petals and see

nothing with the face of a poet really which
is a flower and not a face with
hands
which whisper
This is my beloved my

                        (suddenly in sunlight
he will bow,

and the whole garden will bow)

—as for me, I was welcomed as no son of any king and queen was ever welcomed. Here was my joyous fate and my supreme fortune. If somehow a suggestion of this illimitable blessing should come to you from me, my existence here and now would be justified: otherwise, anything I may say to you will have not the slightest significance. For as surely as each November has its April, mysteries only are significant; and one mystery-of-mysteries creates them all:

nothing false and possible is love
(who's imagined,therefore limitless)
love's to giving as to keeping's give;
as yes is to if,love is to yes

I shall not attempt a description of my mother. But let me try to give you a few glimpses of the most amazing person I've ever met. She came of highly respectable Roxbury stock: so highly respectable (indeed) that one of her distinguished forbears, the Reverend Pitt Clarke, withdrew his grown son by the ear from what we should consider a painfully decorous dance. Nor did Clarke respectability stop there. When my mother's father, who was in business with his father-in-law, affixed (on one occasion) the latter's name to a cheque, that worthy not only sent his son-in-law to the Charles Street jail but obliterated his name from the family archives. My mother told me that all during her childhood she supposed that her father had been hanged. She also assured me that she grew up a shy—or (as we now say) neurotic—girl; who had to be plucked from under sofas whenever friends came to call; and this statement I found almost unbelievable, though she could no more have told a lie than flown over the housetop. For never have I encountered anyone more joyous, anyone healthier in body and mind, anyone so quite incapable of remembering a wrong, or anyone so completely and humanly and unaffectedly generous. Whereas my father had created his Unitarianism (his own father being a Christian of the hellfire variety) she had inherited hers; it was an integral part of herself, she expressed it as she breathed and as she smiled. The two indispensable factors in life, my mother always maintained, were "health and a sense of humor." And although her health eventually failed her, she kept her sense of humor to the beginning.

It isn't often you meet a true heroine. I have the honour to be a true heroine's son. My father and mother were coming up from Cambridge to New Hampshire, one day, in their newly purchased automobile—an aircooled Franklin, with an ash frame. As they neared the Ossippees, snow fell. My mother was driving; and, left to herself, would never have paused for such a trifle as snow. But as the snow increased, my father made her stop while he got out and wiped the windshield. Then he got in; and she drove on. Some minutes later, a locomotive cut the car in half, killing my father instantly. When two brakemen jumped from the halted train, they saw a woman standing—dazed but erect—beside a mangled machine; with blood "spouting" (as the older said to me) out of her head. One of her hands (the younger added) kept feeling of her dress, as if trying to discover why it was wet. These men took my sixty-six year old mother by the arms and tried to lead her toward a nearby farmhouse; but she threw them off, strode straight to my father's body, and directed a group of scared spectators to cover him. When this had been done (and only then) she let them lead her away.

A day later, my sister and I entered a small darkened room in a country hospital. She was still alive—why, the headdoctor couldn't imagine. She wanted only one thing: to join the person she loved most. He was very near her, but she could not quite reach him. We spoke, and she recognized our voices. Gradually her own voice began to understand what its death would mean to these living children of hers; and very gradually a miracle happened. She decided to live. "There's something wrong with my head" she kept telling us faintly; and she didn't mean the fracture of her skull. As days and nights passed, we accidentally discovered that this ghastly wound had been sewn up by candlelight when all the town lights went out at once. But the headdoctor had no intention of losing his patient—"move her?" he cried "impossible! It would kill her just to sit up" and several centuries wandered away before we found a method of overruling him. When the ambulance arrived, ready to transfer my mother to a big Boston hospital, she was sitting up (fully dressed and smiling) by the entrance-door. She admired the ambulance, conversed cheerfully with its chauffeur, and refused to lie down because by so doing she'd miss the scenery en route. We shot through towns and tore through cities. "I like going fast" she told us; beaming. At last came the goal. After an interminable time in an operatingroom—where (we learned later) she insisted on watching in a handmirror whatever was happening, while a great brain-surgeon removed a piece of bone and carefully cleansed the wound—up came my mother in a wheelchair; very erect, and waving triumphantly a small bottle in which (at her urgent request) he'd placed the dirt and grime and splinters of whose existence his predecessor had been blissfully unaware. "You see?" she cried to us, smiling "I was right!"

And, though the wound had later to be reopened, she came out of that hospital in record time; recovered completely at home in a few months—attending, now and then, a nearby meeting of The Society of Friends—then boarded a train alone for New York, and began working as a volunteer for the Travellers' Aid in the Grand Central Station. "I'm tough!" was her dauntless comment when we tried to express our amazement and our joy.

My mother loved poetry; and copied most of the poems she loved best into a little book which was never far from her.

Some of these poems I also love best. And one of them I shall now try—in the quarter-hour remaining—to read you. It is William Wordsworth's Ode, entitled Intimations Of Immortality From Recollections Of Early Childhood; and prefaced by these three lines:

The Child is father of the Man;
And I could wish my days to be
Bound each to each by natural piety.

There was a time when meadow, grove, and stream,
The earth, and every common sight,
                To me did seem
            Apparell'd in celestial light,
The glory and the freshness of a dream.
It is not now as it hath been of yore;—
            Turn wheresoe'er I may,
                By night or day,
The things which I have seen I now can see no more.

            The rainbow comes and goes,
            And lovely is the rose;
            The moon doth with delight
        Look round her when the heavens are bare;
            Waters on a starry night
            Are beautiful and fair;
        The sunshine is a glorious birth;
        But yet I know, where'er I go,
That there hath pass'd away a glory from the earth.

Now, while the birds thus sing a joyous song,
            And while the young lambs bound
                As to the tabor's sound,
To me alone there came a thought of grief:
A timely utterance gave that thought relief,
            And I again am strong:
The cataracts blow their trumpets from the steep;
No more shall grief of mine the season wrong;
I hear the echoes through the mountains throng,
The winds come to me from the fields of sleep,
            And all the earth is gay;
                Land and sea
        Give themselves up to jollity,
            And with the heart of May
        Doth every beast keep holiday;—
            Thou Child of Joy,
Shout round me, let me hear thy shouts, thou happy Shepherd-boy!

Ye blessèd creatures, I have heard the call
        Ye to each other make; I see

The heavens laugh with you in your jubilee;
    My heart is at your festival,
    My head hath its coronal,
The fullness of your bliss, I feel—I feel it all.
        O evil day! if I were sullen
        While Earth herself is adorning,
            This sweet May-morning,
        And the children are culling
            On every side,
        In a thousand valleys far and wide,
        Fresh flowers; while the sun shines warm,
And the babe leaps up on his mother's arm:—
        I hear, I hear, with joy I hear!
    —But there's a tree, of many, one,
A single field which I have look'd upon,
Both of them speak of something that is gone:
        The pansy at my feet
        Doth the same tale repeat:
Whither is fled the visionary gleam?
Where is it now, the glory and the dream?

Our birth is but a sleep and a forgetting:
The Soul that rises with us, our life's Star,
        Hath had elsewhere its setting,
            And cometh from afar:
        Not in entire forgetfulness,
        And not in utter nakedness,
But trailing clouds of glory do we come
        From God, who is our home:
Heaven lies about us in our infancy!
Shades of the prison-house begin to close
        Upon the growing Boy,
But he beholds the light, and whence it flows,
        He sees it in his joy;
The Youth, who daily farther from the east
    Must travel, still is Nature's priest,
        And by the vision splendid
        Is on his way attended;
At length the Man perceives it die away,
And fade into the light of common day.

Earth fills her lap with pleasures of her own;
　　Yearnings she hath in her own natural kind;
And, even with something of a mother's mind,
　　　　And no unworthy aim,
　　The homely nurse doth all she can
To make her foster-child, her inmate Man,
　　Forget the glories he hath known,
And that imperial palace whence he came.

Behold the Child among his new-born blisses,
A six years' darling of a pigmy size!
See, where 'mid work of his own hand he lies,
Fretted by sallies of his mother's kisses,
With light upon him from his father's eyes!
See, at his feet, some little plan or chart,
Some fragment from his dream of human life,
Shaped by himself with newly-learnèd art;
　　　　A wedding or a festival,
　　　　A mourning or a funeral;
　　　　And this hath now his heart,
　　And unto this he frames his song:
　　　　Then will he fit his tongue
To dialogues of business, love, or strife;
　　　　But it will not be long
　　　　Ere this be thrown aside,
　　　　And with new joy and pride
The little actor cons another part;
Filling from time to time his 'humorous stage'
With all the Persons, down to palsied Age,
That Life brings with her in her equipage;
　　　　As if his whole vocation
　　　　Were endless imitation.

Thou, whose exterior semblance doth belie
　　　　Thy soul's immensity;
Thou best philosopher, who yet dost keep
Thy heritage, thou eye among the blind,
That, deaf and silent, read'st the eternal deep,
Haunted for ever by the eternal mind,—

Mighty prophet! Seer blest!
On whom those truths do rest,
Which we are toiling all our lives to find,
In darkness lost, the darkness of the grave;
Thou, over whom thy Immortality
Broods like the Day, a master o'er a slave,
A presence which is not to be put by;
Thou little Child, yet glorious in the might
Of heaven-born freedom on thy being's height,
Why with such earnest pains dost thou provoke
The years to bring the inevitable yoke,
Thus blindly with thy blessedness at strife?
Full soon thy soul shall have her earthly freight,
And custom lie upon thee with a weight,
Heavy as frost, and deep almost as life!

O joy! that in our embers
Is something that doth live,
That nature yet remembers
What was so fugitive!
The thought of our past years in me doth breed
Perpetual benediction: not indeed
For that which is most worthy to be blest—
Delight and liberty, the simple creed
Of childhood, whether busy or at rest,
With new-fledged hope still fluttering in his breast:—
Not for these I raise
The song of thanks and praise;
But for those obstinate questionings
Of sense and outward things,
Fallings from us, vanishings;
Blank misgivings of a Creature
Moving about in worlds not realized,
High instincts before which our mortal Nature
Did tremble like a guilty thing surprised:
But for those first affections,
Those shadowy recollections,
Which, be they what they may,
Are yet the fountain-light of all our day,
Are yet a master-light of all our seeing;

Uphold us, cherish, and have power to make
Our noisy years seem moments in the being
Of the eternal Silence: truths that wake,
   To perish never:
Which neither listlessness, nor mad endeavour,
   Nor Man nor Boy,
Nor all that is at enmity with joy,
Can utterly abolish or destroy!
  Hence in a season of calm weather
   Though inland far we be,
Our souls have sight of that immortal sea
   Which brought us hither,
   Can in a moment travel thither,
And see the children sport upon the shore,
And hear the mighty waters rolling evermore.

Then sing, ye birds, sing, sing a joyous song!
   And let the young lambs bound
   As to the tabor's sound!
We in thought will join your throng,
   Ye that pipe and ye that play,
   Ye that through your hearts to-day
   Feel the gladness of the May!
What though the radiance which was once so bright
Be now for ever taken from my sight,
  Though nothing can bring back the hour
Of splendour in the grass, of glory in the flower;
   We will grieve not, rather find
   Strength in what remains behind;
   In the primal sympathy
   Which having been must ever be;
   In the soothing thoughts that spring
   Out of human suffering;
   In the faith that looks through death,
In years that bring the philosophic mind.

And O ye Fountains, Meadows, Hills, and Groves,
Forebode not any severing of our loves!
Yet in my heart of hearts I feel your might;

I only have relinquish'd one delight
To live beneath your more habitual sway.
I love the brooks which down their channels fret,
Even more than when I tripp'd lightly as they;
The innocent brightness of a new-born Day
              Is lovely yet;
The clouds that gather round the setting sun
Do take a sober colouring from an eye
That hath kept watch o'er man's mortality;
Another race hath been, and other palms are won.
Thanks to the human heart by which we live,
Thanks to its tenderness, its joys, and fears,
To me the meanest flower that blows can give
Thoughts that do often lie too deep for tears.

i &

their son

NONLECTURE TWO

You will perhaps pardon me, as a nonlecturer, if I begin my second nonlecture with an almost inconceivable assertion: I was born at home.

For the benefit of those of you who can't imagine what the word "home" implies, or what a home could possibly have been like, I should explain that the idea of home is the idea of privacy. But again—what is privacy? You probably never heard of it. Even supposing that (from time to time) walls exist around you, those walls are no longer walls; they are merest pseudosolidities, perpetually penetrated by the perfectly predatory collective organs of sight and sound. Any apparent somewhere which you may inhabit is always at the mercy of a ruthless and omnivorous everywhere. The notion of a house, as one single definite particular and unique place to come into, from the anywhereish and everywhereish world outside—that notion must strike you as fantastic. You have been brought up to believe that a house, or a universe, or a you, or any other object, is only seemingly solid: really (and you are realists, whom nobody and nothing can deceive) each seeming solidity is a collection of large holes—and, in the case of a house, the larger the holes the better; since the principal function of a modern house is to admit whatever might otherwise remain outside. You haven't the least or feeblest conception of being here, and now, and alone, and yourself. Why (you ask) should anyone want to be here, when (simply by pressing a button) anyone can be in fifty places at once? How could anyone want to be now, when anyone can go whening all over creation at the twist of a knob? What could induce anyone to desire aloneness, when billions of soi-disant dollars are mercifully squandered by a good and great government lest anyone anywhere should ever for a single instant be alone? As for being yourself— why on earth should you be yourself; when instead of being yourself you can be a hundred, or a thousand, or a hundred thousand thousand, other people? The very thought of being oneself in an epoch of interchangeable selves must appear supremely ridiculous.

Fine and dandy: but, so far as I am concerned, poetry and every other art was and is and forever will be strictly and distinctly a question of individuality. If poetry were anything— like dropping an atombomb—which anyone did, anyone could become a poet merely by doing the necessary anything; whatever that anything might or might not entail. But (as it happens) poetry is being, not doing. If you wish to follow, even at a distance, the poet's calling (and here, as always, I speak from my own totally biased and entirely personal point of view) you've got to come out of the measurable doing universe into the immeasurable house of being. I am quite aware that, wherever our socalled civilization has slithered, there's every reward and no punishment for unbeing. But if poetry is your goal, you've got to forget all about punishments and all about rewards and all about selfstyled obligations and duties and responsibilities etcetera ad infinitum and remember one thing only: that it's you—nobody else—who determine your destiny and decide your fate. Nobody else can be alive for you; nor can you be alive for anybody else. Toms can be Dicks and Dicks can be Harrys, but none of them can ever be you. There's the artist's responsibility; and the most awful responsibility on earth. If you can take it, take it—and be. If you can't, cheer up and go about other people's business; and do (or undo) till you drop.

My own home faced the Cambridge world as a finely and solidly constructed mansion, preceded by a large oval lawn and ringed with an imposing white-pine hedge. Just in front of the house itself stood two huge appletrees; and faithfully, every spring, these giants lifted their worlds of fragrance toward the room where I breathed and dreamed. Under one window of this room flourished (in early summer) a garden of magnificent roses: the gift of my parents' dear friend "stubby" Child—who (I learned later) baptized me and who (I still later discovered) was the Child of English And Scottish Ballads. As a baby, I sported a white sweater; on which my mother had embroidered a red H, for Harvard.

Our nearest neighbour, dwelling (at a decent distance) behind us, was Roland Thaxter; primarily the father of my loveliest playmate and ultimately the professor of cryptogamic botany. To our right, on Irving Street, occurred professors James and Royce and Warren; to our left, on Scott Street, transpired professor of economics Taussig. Somewhat back of the Taussig house happened professor Lanman—"known and loved throughout India" as my mother would say, with a pensive smile. She had been slightly astonished by an incident which embellished her official introduction to Mr and Mrs Lanman: the celebrated Sanscrit scholar having, it seems, seized his would-be interlocutor's hand, yanked her aside, and violently whispered "do you see anything peculiar about my wife?"—then (without giving my mother time to reply) "she has new shoes on" professor Lanman hissed "and they hurt her!" I myself experienced astonishment when first witnessing a spectacle which frequently thereafter repeated itself at professor Royce's gate. He came rolling peacefully forth, attained the sidewalk, and was about to turn right and wander up Irving, when Mrs Royce shot out of the house with a piercing cry "Josie! Josie!" waving something stringlike in her dexter fist. Mr Royce politely paused, allowing his spouse to catch up with him; he then shut both eyes, while she snapped around his collar a narrow necktie possessing a permanent bow; his eyes thereupon opened, he bowed, she smiled, he advanced, she retired, and the scene was over. As for professor Taussig, he had a cocker spaniel named Hamlet; and the Taussig family always put Hamlet out when they played their pianola—no doubt the first law of economics—but Hamlet's hearing was excellent, and he yodelled heartrendingly as long as the Hungarian Rhapsody persisted. Genial professor Warren's beautiful wife (whose own beautiful name was Salomé Machado) sometimes came to call on my maternal grandmother; and Salomé always brought her guitar. I remember sitting spellbound on our upstairs porch among appleblossoms, one heavenly spring afternoon, adoring the quick slim fingers of Salomé Machado's exquisite left hand—and I further remember how, as Salomé sang and played, a scarlet tanager alighted in the blossoms; and listened, and disappeared.

One of the many wonderful things about a home is that it can be as lively as you please without ever becoming public. The big Cambridge house was in this respect, as in all other respects, a true home. Although I could be entirely alone when I wished, a varied social life awaited me whenever aloneness palled. A father and mother—later, a sister—two successive grandmothers and an aunt (all three of whom sang, or played the piano, or did both, extremely well) and one uncle, plus three or four hearty and jovial servants, were at my almost unlimited disposal. The servants—and this strikes me as a more than important point—very naturally enjoyed serving: for they were not ignobly irresponsible impersons, they were not shamelessly overpaid and mercilessly manipulated anonymities, they were not pampered and impotent particles of a greedy and joyless collective obscenity. In brief: they were not slaves. Actually, these good and faithful servants (of whom I speak) were precisely everything which no slave can ever be—they were alive; they were loved and loving human beings. From them, a perfect ignoramus could and did learn what any unworld will never begin to begin to so much as suspect: that slavery, and the only slavery, is service without love.

After myself and my father and mother, I loved most dearly my mother's brother George. He was by profession a lawyer, by inclination a bon vivant, and by nature a joyous human being.

When this joyous human being wasn't toiling in his office, or hobnobbing with socalled swells at the Brookline country club, he always became my playfellow. No more innocently good-hearted soul ever kissed the world goodnight; but when it came to literature, bloodthirsty was nothing to him. And (speaking of bloodthirstiness) I here devoutly thank a beneficent Providence for allowing me to live my childhood and my boyhood and even my youth without ever once glimpsing that typical item of an era of at least penultimate confusion—the uncomic nonbook. No paltry supermen, no shadowy space-cadets, no trifling hyperjunglequeens and pantless pantherwomen insulted my virginal imagination. I read or was read, at an early age, the most immemorial myths, the wildest wild animal stories, lots of Scott and quantities of Dickens (including the immortal Pickwick Papers), Robinson Crusoe and The Swiss Family Robinson, Gulliver's Travels, Twenty Thousand Leagues Under The Sea, poetry galore, The Holy Bible, and The Arabian Nights. One city winter I floated through chivalry with Mallory and Froissart: the following country summer—we had by then acquired a farm—I dressed as a Red Indian, slept in a teepee, and almost punctured our best Jersey cow with a random arrow; in emulation of the rightful inhabitants of my wrongful native land.

A gruesome history of the Tower Of London had been con-scientiously compiled by a prominent British prelate, endowed with what would now be termed sadistic trends; and suddenly this fearful opus burgeoned in our midst. Every night after dinner, if George were on deck, he would rub his hands and wink magnificently in my direction and call to my maiden aunt "Jane, let's have some ruddy gore!" whereupon Jane would protestingly join us in the parlour; and George would stealthily produce the opus; and she would blushfully read; and I would cling to the sofa in exquisite terror. We also read—for sheer relaxation—Lorna Doone (with whom I fell sublimely in love) and Treasure Island (as a result of which, the blind pirate Pew followed me upstairs for weeks; while for months, if not years, onelegged John Silver stood just behind me as my trembling fingers fumbled the electric light chain).

Out of Brookline's already mentioned country club, I readily conjured a gorgeous and dangerous play-world: somewhat resembling the three ring circus of the five Ringling brothers; and dedicated by dashing gentlemen to fair ladies and fine horses and other entrancing symbols of luxurious living. George had not been born into this fashionable cosmos, but he loved it so much that he learned to smoke cigars: and if he hadn't learned anything, the cosmos would certainly have welcomed him for his own abundant self's sake. His own abundant self wrote vers de société; which he recited at orgies or banquets— I was never sure which—but also, for my benefit, chez lui. And no sooner had George discovered my liking for verse than he presented me with an inestimable treasure entitled The Rhymester—opening which totally unostentatious masterpiece, I entered my third poetic period.

Poetic period number one had been nothing if not individualistic; as two almost infantile couplets, combining fearless expression with keen observation, amply testify. The first of these primeval authenticities passionately exclaims

O,the pretty birdie,O;
with his little toe,toe,toe!

while the second mercilessly avers

there was a little farder
and he made his mudder harder

—but, alas! a moribund mental cloud soon obscured my vital psychic sky. The one and only thing which mattered about any poem (so ran my second poetic period's credo) was what the poem said; it's socalled meaning. A good poem was a poem which did good, and a bad poem was a poem which didn't: Julia Ward Howe's Battle Hymn Of The Republic being a good poem because it helped free the slaves. Armed with this ethical immutability, I composed canticles of comfort on behalf of the griefstricken relatives of persons recently deceased; I implored healthy Christians to assist poor-whites afflicted with The Curse Of The Worm (short for hookworm); and I exhorted right-minded patriots to abstain from dangerous fireworks on the 4th of July. Thus it will be seen that, by the year 1900, one growing American boy had reached exactly that stage of "intellectual development" beyond which every ungrowing Marxist adult of today is strictly forbidden, on pain of physical disappearance, ever to pass.

The Rhymester diverted my eager energies from what to how: from substance to structure. I learned that there are all kinds of intriguing verse-forms, chiefly French; and that each of these forms can and does exist in and of itself, apart from the use to which you or I may not or may put it. A rondel is a rondel, irrespective of any idea which it may be said to embody; and whatever a ballade may be about, it is always a ballade—never a villanelle or a rondeau. With this welcome revelation, the mental cloud aforesaid ignominiously dissolved; and my psychic sky joyfully reappeared, more vital even than before.

One ever memorable day, our ex-substantialist (deep in structural meditation) met head-on professor Royce; who was rolling peacefully home from a lecture. "Estlin" his courteous and gentle voice hazarded "I understand that you write poetry." I blushed. "Are you perhaps" he inquired, regarding a particular leaf of a particular tree "acquainted with the sonnets of

Dante Gabriel Rossetti?" I blushed a different blush and shook
an ignorant head. "Have you a moment?" he shyly suggested,
less than half looking at me; and just perceptibly appended "I
rather imagine you might enjoy them." Shortly thereafter, sage
and ignoramus were sitting opposite each other in a diminutive
study (marvellously smelling of tobacco and cluttered with
student notebooks of a menacing bluish shade)—the ignoramus
listening, enthralled; the sage intoning, lovingly and beautifully,
his favorite poems. And very possibly (although I don't, as
usual, know) that is the reason—or more likely the unreason—
I've been writing sonnets ever since.

En route to a university whose name begins with H, our unhero
attended four Cambridge schools: the first, private—where
everybody was extraordinarily kind; and where (in addition to
learning nothing) I burst into tears and nosebleeds—the other
three, public; where I flourished like the wicked and learned
what the wicked learn, and where almost nobody cared about
somebody else. Two figures emerge from this almost: a Miss
Maria Baldwin and a Mr Cecil Derry. Miss Baldwin, the dark
lady mentioned in my first nonlecture (and a lady if ever a
lady existed) was blessed with a delicious voice, charming man-
ners, and a deep understanding of children. Never did any
demidivine dictator more gracefully and easily rule a more
unruly and less graceful populace. Her very presence emanated
an honour and a glory: the honour of spiritual freedom—no
mere freedom from—and the glory of being, not (like most
extant mortals) really undead, but actually alive. From her I
marvellingly learned that the truest power is gentleness. Concerning Mr. Derry, let me say only that he was (and for me will
always remain) one of those blessing and blessed spirits who
deserve the name of teacher: predicates who are utterly in love
with their subject; and who, because they would gladly die for
it, are living for it gladly. From him I learned (and am still
learning) that gladness is next to godliness. He taught me Greek.

This may be as apt a moment as any to state that in the world of my boyhood—long, long ago; before time was space and Oedipus was a complex and religion was the opiate of the people and pigeons had learned to play pingpong—social stratification not merely existed but luxuriated. All women were not, as now, ladies; a gentleman was a gentleman; and a mucker (as the professorial denizens of Irving and Scott streets knew full well: since their lofty fragment of Cambridge almost adjoined plebeian Somerville) was a mucker. Being myself a professor's (& later a clergyman's) son, I had every socalled reason to accept these conventional distinctions without cavil; yet for some unreason I didn't. The more implacably a virtuous Cambridge drew me toward what might have been her bosom, the more sure I felt that soi-disant respectability comprised nearly everything which I couldn't respect, and the more eagerly I explored sinful Somerville. But while sinful Somerville certainly possessed a bosom (in fact, bosoms) she also possessed fists which hit below the belt and arms which threw snowballs containing small rocks. Little by little and bruise by teacup, my doubly disillusioned spirit made an awe-inspiring discovery; which (on more than several occasions) has prevented me from wholly misunderstanding socalled humanity: the discovery, namely, that all groups, gangs, and collectivities—no matter how apparently disparate—are fundamentally alike; and that what makes any world go round is not the trivial difference between a Somerville and a Cambridge, but the immeasurable difference between either of them and individuality. Whether this discovery is valid for you, I can't pretend to say: but I can and do say, without pretending, that it's true for me—inasmuch as I've found (and am still finding) authentic individuals in the most varied environments conceivable. Nor will anything ever persuade me that, by turning Somerville into Cambridge or Cambridge into Somerville or both into neither, anybody can make an even slightly better world. Better worlds (I suggest) are born, not made; and their birthdays are the birthdays of individuals. Let us pray always for individuals; never for worlds. "He who would do good to another" cries the poet and painter William Blake "must do it in Minute Particulars"—and probably many of you are familiar with this greatly pitying line. But I'll wager that not three of you could quote me the line which follows it

General Good is the plea of the scoundrel, hypocrite, &flatterer

for that deeply terrible line spells the doom of all unworlds; whatever their slogans and their strategies, whoever their heroes or their villains.

Only a butterfly's glide from my home began a mythical domain of semiwilderness; separating cerebral Cambridge and orchidaceous Somerville. Deep in this magical realm of Between stood a palace, containing Harvard University's far-famed Charles Eliot Norton: and lowly folk, who were neither professors nor professors' children, had nicknamed the district Norton's Woods. Here, as a very little child, I first encountered that mystery who is Nature; here my enormous smallness entered Her illimitable being; and here someone actually infinite or impossibly alive—someone who might almost (but not quite) have been myself—wonderingly wandered the mortally immortal complexities of Her beyond imagining imagination

O sweet spontaneous
earth how often have
the
doting

        fingers of
prurient philosophers pinched
and
poked

thee
,has the naughty thumb
of science prodded
thy

    beauty   .how
often have religions taken
thee upon their scraggy knees
squeezing and

buffeting thee that thou mightest conceive
gods
    (but
true

to the incomparable
couch of death thy
rhythmic
lover

      thou answerest

them only with

           spring)

—later, this beyond imagining imagination revealed a not
believably mountaining ocean, at Lynn; and, in New Hampshire, oceaning miraculously mountains. But the wonder of my
first meeting with Herself is with me now; and also with me is
the coming (obedient to Her each resurrection) of a roguish
and resistless More Than Someone: Whom my deepest selves
unfailingly recognized, though His disguise protected him from
all the world

in Just-
spring   when the world is mud-
luscious the little
lame balloonman

whistles   far   and wee

and eddyandbill come
running from marbles and
piracies and it's
spring

when the world is puddle-wonderful

the queer
old balloonman whistles
far   and   wee
and bettyandisbel come dancing

from hop-scotch and jump-rope and

it's
spring
and
   the

        goat-footed

balloonMan   whistles
far
and
wee

this Turbulent Individual Incognito must have rendered his
disciple even less law-abiding than usual; for I vividly remember
being chased (with two charming little girls) out of the tallest
and thickest of several palatial lilac bushes: our pursuer being a
frantic scarecrow-demon masquerading as my good friend
Bernard Magrath, professor Charles Eliot Norton's gifted coachman. But why not? Then it was spring; and in spring anything
may happen.

Absolutely anything.

In honour of which truth (and in recognition of the fact that, as recent events have shown, almost anything can happen in November) let me now present, without socalled criticism or comment, five springtime celebrations which I love even more than if they were my own—first, a poem by Thomas Nashe; second, the opening of Chaucer's Canterbury Tales; third, a chorus from Atalanta in Calydon by Swinburne; fourth, a rondel by Charles d'Orléans; and finally, a song by Shakespeare. Item: if these celebrations don't sing (instead of speaking) for themselves, please blame me; not them.

Spring, the sweete spring, is the yeres pleasant King,
Then bloomes eche thing, then maydes daunce in a ring,
Cold doeth not sting, the pretty birds doe sing,
Cuckow, jugge, jugge, pu we, to witta woo.

The Palme and May make countrey houses gay,
Lambs friske and play, the Shepherds pype all day,
And we heare aye birds tune this merry lay,
Cuckow, jugge, jugge, pu we, to witta woo.

The fields breathe sweete, the dayzies kisse our feete,
Young lovers meete, old wives a sunning sit;
In every streete, these tunes our eares doe greete,
Cuckow, jugge, jugge, pu we, to witta woo.
    Spring, the sweete spring.

Whan that Aprille with his shoures sote
The droghte of Marche hath perced to the rote,
And bathed every veyne in swich licour,
Of which vertu engendred is the flour;
Whan Zephirus eek with his swete breeth
Inspired hath in every holt and heeth
The tendre croppes, and the yonge sonne
Hath in the Ram his halfe cours y-ronne,
And smale fowles maken melodye,
That slepen al the night with open yë,
(So priketh hem nature in hir corages):
Than longen folk to goon on pilgrimages
(And palmers for to seken straunge strondes)
To ferne halwes, couthe in sondry londes;
And specially, from every shires ende
Of Engelond, to Caunterbury they wende,
The holy blisful martir for to seke,
That hem hath holpen, whan that they were seke.

When the hounds of spring are on winter's traces,
    The mother of months in meadow or plain
Fills the shadows and windy places
    With lisp of leaves and ripple of rain;
And the brown bright nightingale amorous
Is half assuaged for Itylus,
For the Thracian ships and the foreign faces.
    The tongueless vigil, and all the pain.

Come with bows bent and with emptying of quivers,
    Maiden most perfect, lady of light,
With a noise of winds and many rivers,
    With a clamour of waters, and with might;
Bind on thy sandals, O thou most fleet,
Over the splendour and speed of thy feet;
For the faint east quickens, the wan west shivers,
    Round the feet of the day and the feet of the night.

Where shall we find her, how shall we sing to her,
    Fold our hands round her knees, and cling?
O that man's heart were as fire and could spring to her,
    Fire, or the strength of the streams that spring!
For the stars and the winds are unto her
As raiment, as songs of the harp-player;
For the risen stars and the fallen cling to her,
    And the southwest-wind and the west-wind sing.

For winter's rains and ruins are over,
    And all the season of snows and sins;
The days dividing lover and lover,
    The light that loses, the night that wins;
And time remember'd is grief forgotten,
And frosts are slain and flowers begotten,
And in green underwood and cover
    Blossom by blossom the Spring begins.

The full streams feed on flower of rushes,
    Ripe grasses trammel a travelling foot,
The faint fresh flame of the young year flushes
    From leaf to flower and flower to fruit;

And fruit and leaf are as gold and fire,
And the oat is heard above the lyre,
And the hoofed heel of a satyr crushes
    The chestnut-husk at the chestnut-root.

And Pan by noon and Bacchus by night,
    Fleeter of foot than the fleet-foot kid,
Follows with dancing and fills with delight
    The Mænad and the Bassarid;
And soft as lips that laugh and hide
The laughing leaves of the trees divide,
And screen from seeing and leave in sight
    The god pursuing, the maiden hid.

The ivy falls with the Bacchanal's hair
    Over her eyebrows hiding her eyes;
The wild vine slipping down leaves bare
    Her bright breast shortening into sighs;
The wild vine slips with the weight of its leaves,
But the berried ivy catches and cleaves
To the limbs that glitter, the feet that scare
    The wolf that follows, the fawn that flies.

Le temps a laissié son manteau
De vent, de froidure et de pluye,
Et s'est vestu de brouderie
De souleil luisant cler et beau.

Il n'y a beste ne oyseau
Qu'en son jargon ne chante ou crie;
Le temps a laissié son manteau
De vent, de froidure et de pluye.

Rivière, fontaine et ruisseau
Portent, en livrée jolie,
Gouttes d'argen d'or faverie,
Chascun s'abille de nouveau;
Le temps a laissié son manteau
De vent, de froidure et de pluye.

It was a Lover and his lasse,
    With a hey, and a ho, and a hey nonino:
That o'er the greene corne field did passe,
    In the spring time, the onely pretty ring time,
When Birds do sing, hey ding a ding, ding.
Sweet Lovers love the spring.

Betweene the acres of the Rie,
    With a hey, and a ho, and a hey nonino:
These prettie Countryfolk would lie,
    In the spring time, the onely pretty ring time,
When Birds do sing, hey ding a ding, ding.
Sweet Lovers love the spring.

This Carroll they began that houre,
    With a hey, and a ho, and a hey nonino:
How that a life was but a Flower,
    In the spring time, the onely pretty ring time,
When Birds do sing, hey ding a ding, ding.
Sweet Lovers love the spring.

And therefore take the present time
    With a hey, and a ho, and a hey nonino:
For love is crownèd with the prime,
    In the spring time, the onely pretty ring time,
When Birds do sing, hey ding a ding, ding.
Sweet Lovers love the spring.

i &

selfdiscovery

NONLECTURE THREE

In the course of my first nonlecture, I affirmed that—for me—personality is a mystery; that mysteries alone are significant; and that love is the mystery-of-mysteries who creates them all. During my second outspokenness, I contrasted the collective behaviour of unchildren with the mystery of individuality; and gave (or attempted to give) you one particular child's earliest glimpse of a mystery called nature. Now I shall try to communicate—clumsily, no doubt, but honestly—certain attitudes and reactions surrounding the mystery of transition from which emerged a poet and painter named EECummings.

As it was my miraculous fortune to have a true father and a true mother, and a home which the truth of their love made joyous, so—in reaching outward from this love and this joy—I was marvellously lucky to touch and seize a rising and striving world; a reckless world, filled with the curiosity of life herself; a vivid and violent world welcoming every challenge; a world worth hating and adoring and fighting and forgiving: in brief, a world which was a world. This inwardly immortal world of my adolescence recoils to its very roots whenever, nowadays, I see people who've been endowed with legs crawling on their chins after quote security unquote. "Security?" I marvel to myself "what is that? Something negative, undead, suspicious and suspecting; an avarice and an avoidance; a self-surrendering meanness of withdrawal; a numerable complacency and an innumerable cowardice. Who would be 'secure'? Every and any slave. No free spirit ever dreamed of 'security'—or, if he did, he laughed; and lived to shame his dream. No whole sinless sinful sleeping waking breathing human creature ever was (or could be) bought by, and sold for, 'security.' How monstrous and how feeble seems some unworld which would rather have its too than eat its cake!"

Jehova buried,Satan dead,
do fearers worship Much & Quick;
badness not being felt as bad,
itself thinks goodness what is meek;
obey says toc,submit says tic,
Eternity's a Five Year Plan:
if Joy with Pain shall hang in hock
who dares to call himself a man?

For the benefit of any heretical members of my audience who
do not regard manhood as a barbarous myth propagated by
sinister powers envisaging the subjugation of womankind, let me
(at this point) cheerfully risk a pair of perhaps not boring
anecdotes.

Back in the days of dog-eat-dog—my first anecdote begins—
there lived a playboy; whose father could easily have owned the
original superskyscraper-de-luxe: a selfstyled Cathedral Of
Commerce, endowed with every impetus to relaxation; not
excluding ultraelevators which (on the laudable assumption
that even machinery occasionally makes mistakes) were regu-
larly tested. Testing an ultraelevator meant that its car was
brought clean up, deprived of safety devices, and dropped.
As the car hurtled downward, a column of air confined by the
elevator shaft became more and more compressed; until (assuming that nothing untoward happened) it broke the car's fall
completely—or so I was told by somebody who should know.
At any rate, young Mr X was in the habit not only of attending
these salubrious ceremonies, but of entering each about-to-be-
dropped car, and of dropping with it as far and as long as the
laws of a preEinsteinian universe permitted. Eventually, of
course, somebody who shouldn't know telephoned a newspaper;
which sent a reporter: who (after scarcely believing his senses)
asked the transcender of Adam point-blank why he fell so often.
Our playful protagonist shrugged his well-tailored shoulders—

"for fun" he said simply; adding (in a strictly confidential undertone) "and it's wonderful for a hangover."

Here, I feel, we have the male American stance of my adolescence; or (if you prefer) the adolescent American male stance of what some wit once nicknamed a "lost generation": whereof— let me hastily append—the present speaker considers himself no worthy specimen. My point, however, isn't that many of us were even slightly heroic; and is that few of us declined a gamble. I don't think we enjoyed courting disaster. I do feel we liked being born.

And now let me give you my second anecdote: which concerns (appropriately enough) not a single human being whose name I forget, but a millionary mishmash termed The Public.

Rather recently—in New York City—an old college chum, whom I hadn't beheld for decades, appeared out of nowhere to tell me he was through with civilization. It seems that ever since Harvard he'd been making (despite all sorts of panics and panaceas) big money as an advertising writer; and this remarkable feat unutterably depressed him. After profound meditation, he concluded that America, and the world which she increasingly dominated, couldn't really be as bad as she and it looked through an advertising writer's eyes; and he promptly determined to seek another view—a larger view; in fact, the largest view obtainable. Bent on obtaining this largest obtainable view of America and America's world, my logical expal wangled an appointment with a subsubeditor of a magazine (if magazine it may be called) possessing the largest circulation on earth: a periodical whose each emanation appears simultaneously in almost every existing human language. Our intrepid explorer then straightened his tie, took six deep breaths, cleared his throat, swam right up, presented his credentials, and was politely requested to sit down. He sat down. "Now listen" the subsubeditor suggested "if you're thinking of working with us, you'd better know The Three Rules." "And what" my friend cheerfully inquired "are The Three Rules?" "The Three Rules" explained his mentor "are: first, eight to eighty; second, anybody can do it; and third, makes you feel better." "I don't quite understand" my friend confessed. "Perfectly simple" his interlocutor assured him. "Our first Rule means that every article we publish must appeal to anybody, man woman or child, between the ages of eight and eighty years—is that clear?" My friend said it was indeed clear. "Second" his enlightener continued "every article we publish must convince any reader of the article that he or she could do whatever was done by the person about whom the article was written. Suppose (for instance) you were writing about Lindbergh, who had just flown the Atlantic ocean for the first time in history, with nothing but unlimited nerve and a couple of chicken (or ham was it?) sandwiches—do you follow me? "I'm ahead of you" my friend murmured. "Remembering Rule number two" the subsub went on "you'd impress upon your readers' minds, over and over again, the fact that (after all) there wouldn't have been anything extraordinary about Lindbergh if he hadn't been just a human being like every single one of them. See?" "I see" said my friend grimly. "Third" the subsub intoned "we'll imagine you're describing a record-breaking Chinese flood—millions of poor unfortunate men and women and little children and helpless babies drowning and drowned; millions more perishing of slow starvation: suffering inconceivable, untold agonies, and so forth—well, any reader of this article must feel definitely and distinctly better, when she or he finishes the article, than when he or she began it." "Sounds a trifle difficult" my friend hazarded. "Don't be silly" the oracle admonished. "All you've got to do, when you're through with your horrors, is to close by saying: but (thanks to an all-merciful Providence) we Americans, with our high standard of living and our Christian ideals, will never be subjected to such inhuman conditions; as long as the Stars and Stripes triumphantly float over one nation indivisible, with liberty and justice for all—get me?" "I get you" said my disillusioned friend. "Good bye."

So ends the second anecdote. You may believe it or not, as you wish. As far as I'm concerned, it's the unbelievable—but also unquestionable—selfportrait of a one hundred and one percent pseudoworld: in which truth has become televisionary, in which goodness means not hurting people, and in which beauty is shoppe. Just (or unjust) how any species of authentic individualism could stem from such a collective quagmire, I don't—as always—know; but here are four lines of a poem which didn't:

(While you and i have lips and voices which
are for kissing and to sing with
who cares if some oneeyed son of a bitch
invents an instrument to measure Spring with?

As regards my own self-finding, I have to thank first of all that institution whose initial I flaunted unknowingly during my very earliest days. Officially, Harvard presented me with a smattering of languages and sciences; with a glimpse of Homer, a more than glimpse of Aeschylus Sophocles Euripides and Aristophanes, and a deep glance at Dante and Shakespeare. Unofficially, she gave me my first taste of independence: and the truest friends any man will ever enjoy. The taste of independence came during my senior year, when I was so lucky as to receive a room by myself in the Yard—for living in the Yard was then an honour, not a compulsion; and this honour very properly reserved itself for seniors, who might conceivably appreciate it. Hitherto I had ostensibly lived at home; which meant that intimate contacts with the surrounding world were somewhat periculous. Now I could roam that surrounding world sans peur, if not sans reproche: and I lost no time in doing so. A town called Boston, thus observed, impressed my

unsophisticated spirit as the mecca of all human endeavors—
and be it added that, in this remote era, Boston had her points.
Well do I recall how our far from hero (backed by the most
physically imposing of his acquaintances) dared a stifling dump
near Howard Street, denominated Mother Shannon's; and how
we stopped short, to avoid treading on several spreadeagled
sailors; and how my backer, with irreproachable nonchalance,
exchanged a brace of dollar bills for two tumblers of something
even viler than honest Jack Delaney served during soi-disant
prohibition; and finally how, having merely sampled our
nonbeverages, we successfully attained Scollay Square—to be
greeted by the dispassionate drone of a pintsize pimp, conspicu-
ously stationed on the populous sidewalk under a blaze of movie
bulbs and openly advertising two kinds of love for twenty-five
cents each. Moreover that distant Boston comprised such
authentic incarnations of genius as Bernhardt, whose each
intonation propitiated demons and angels; Pavlova, who danced
a ditty called Nix On The Glowworm into the most absolute
piece of aristocracy since Ming; and a lady of parts (around
whose waist any man's hand immediately dreamed it could go
three times) named Polaire. Those were the days (and nights)
of The Turkey Trot and The Bunny Hug; of Everybody's
Doing It, Alexander's Ragtime Band, Has Anybody Here
Seen Kelly, There's A Little Bit Of Bad In Every Good Little
Girl, On The Banks Of The Saskatchewan, and Here Comes
My Daddy Now (O Pop, O Pop, O Pop, O Pop). Nothing
could exceed the artistry of Washington Street bartenders, who
positively enjoyed constructing impeccable Pousse-Cafés in
the midst of Ward Eights and Hop Toads; nor could anything
approach the courtesy of Woodcock waiters, who never obeyed
any ring but your own and always knocked twice before entering. I am further indebted to Boston town for making me
acquainted (and in no uncertain manner) with the sinister
splendors of censorship. One evening, The Old Howard would
be As Is; the next, you guessed you were embracing a funeral.

When Miss Gertrude Hoffman brought her lissome self and her willowy girls to Boston, they and she were violently immersed in wrist-and-ankle-length underwear. A local tobacconist drew jail for selling a box of cigars adorned with the usual gauzily apparelled but unmistakably symbolic females—and vainly did an outraged lawyer object that his client was happily married. Meanwhile, watching-and-warding Mr Sumner's matchless collection of indecent items constituted a favorite topic of conversation with high and low alike. But if the predations of puritanism astonished me nearly forty years ago, I was recently more than amazed to learn that you cannot now show a woman's entire breast in any American moviehouse unless she isn't (to coin a plagiarism) white. Verily, democracy unquote is a strange disease: nor (I submit) can any human being help sympathizing, in his or her heart of hearts, with the bad bald poet who sings

  come(all you mischief-
hatchers hatch
mischief)all you

 guilty
  scamper(you bastards throw dynamite)
   let knowings magic
   with bright credos each divisible fool

 (life imitate gossip fear unlife
mean
 -ness,and
  to succeed in not
   dying)

  Is will still occur;birds disappear
  becomingly:a thunderbolt compose poems
not because harm symmetry
  earthquakes starfish(but
   because nobody
    can sell the Moon to The)moon

Let us now consider friendship.

Through Harvard, I met Scofield Thayer; and at Harvard, Sibley Watson—two men who subsequently transformed a dogooding periodical called The Dial into a firstrate magazine of the fine arts; and together fought the eternal fight of selfhood against mobism, the immortal battle of beauty against ugliness. It would not even slightly surprise me to learn that most of you have remained, till now, quite unaware of the existence of these literally heroic individuals and of their actually unparalleled achievement. Never have I seen courage and courtesy, taste and intelligence, prodigious patience and incredible generosity, quite so jealously mistrusted or so basely misprized or so savagely detested as by The Dial's detractors. Even today, more than twenty years after this true and noble adventure's culmination, the adventurers' chastisement continues—through such a conspiracy of silence on the part of America's intellectual gangsters as would be ludicrous if it were not abominable; nor will that chastisement begin to diminish while general good outflanks minute particulars and spiritual treachery is the order of the unday.

At Harvard (moreover) I met Stewart Mitchell, who soon became editor-in-chief of our university's only serious undergraduate magazine—The Monthly—and was subsequently managing editor of The Dial; John Dos Passos, through whose devoted efforts a dangerous compilation known as Eight Harvard Poets appeared; and S Foster Damon, who opened my eyes and ears not merely to Domenico Theotocopuli and William Blake, but to all ultra (at that moment) modern music and poetry and painting. Nor can or do I forget Theodore Miller; who gladly brought me such treasures as the exquisite

lugete, o Veneres Cupidinesque
et quantumst hominum venustiorum

of Catullus; the sublime

labuntur anni; nec pietas moram
rugis et instanti senectae
adferet, indomitaeque morti

of Horace; and Sappho's magically luminous invocation

ποικιλόθρον', ἀθάνατ' 'Αφρόδιτα

but the token of whose most memorable kindness was a volume
combining poems and letters by that glorious human being who
confessed

I am certain of nothing but of the holiness of the Heart's affections,
and the truth of Imagination.

Whereupon—deep in those heights of psychic sky which had
greeted my boyish escape from moralism—an unknown and
unknowable bird began singing.

After Harvard, I thank (for selfdiscovery) a phenomenon and
a miracle. The phenomenon was a telemicroscopic chimera,
born of the satanic rape of matter by mind; a phallic female
phantasm, clothed in thunderous anonymity and adorned
with colossally floating spiderwebs of traffic; a stark irresistibly
stupendous newness, mercifully harboring among its pitilessly
premeditated spontaneities immemorial races and nations

by god i want above fourteenth

fifth's deep purring biceps,the mystic screetch
of Broadway,the trivial stink of rich

frail firm asinine life
                    (i pant

for what's below. The singer. Wall. i want
the perpendicular lips the insane teeth
the vertical grin

                    give me the Square in spring,
the little barbarous Greenwich perfumed fake

and most,the futile fooling labyrinth
where noisy colours stroll . . . and the Baboon

sniggering insipidities while. i sit,sipping
singular anisettes as. One opaque
big girl jiggles thickly hips to the canoun

but Hassan chuckles seeing the Greeks breathe)

in New York I also breathed: and as if for the first time.

The truly first of first times was (however) still to come. It
arrived with a socalled war. Being neither warrior nor consci-
entiousobjector, saint nor hero, I embarked for France as an
ambulancedriver. And as my earliest taste of independence had
been excelled by the banquet which I later sampled among
Manhattan's skyscrapers, so was that banquet surpassed by the
freedom which I now tasted:

Paris;this April sunset completely utters
utters serenely silently a cathedral

before whose upward lean magnificent face
the streets turn young with rain

two realms, elsewhere innately hostile, here cordially coexisted—each (by its very distinctness) intensifying the other—nor could I possibly have imagined either a loveliness so fearlessly of the moment or so nobly beautiful a timelessness. Three thousand oceanic miles away and some terrestrial years before, a son of New England had observed those realms bitterly struggling for dominion: then, as a guest of verticality, our impuritan had attended the overwhelming triumph of the temporal realm. Now, I participated in an actual marriage of material with immaterial things; I celebrated an immediate reconciling of spirit and flesh, forever and now, heaven and earth. Paris was for me precisely and complexly this homogeneous duality: this accepting transcendence; this living and dying more than death or life. Whereas—by the very act of becoming its improbably gigantic self—New York had reduced mankind to a tribe of pygmies, Paris (in each shape and gesture and avenue and cranny of her being) was continuously expressing the humanness of humanity. Everywhere I sensed a miraculous presence, not of mere children and women and men, but of living human beings; and the fact that I could scarcely understand their language seemed irrelevant, since the truth of our momentarily mutual aliveness created an imperishable communion. While (at the hating touch of some madness called La Guerre) a once rising and striving world toppled into withering hideously smithereens, love rose in my heart like a sun and beauty blossomed in my life like a star. Now, finally and first, I was myself: a temporal citizen of eternity; one with all human beings born and unborn.

Thus through an alma mater whose scholastic bounty appeared the smallest of her blessings—and by way of those even more munificent institutions of learning, New York and Paris—our ignoramus reaches his supreme indebtedness. Last but most, I thank for my self-finding certain beautiful givers of illimitable gladness

whose any mystery makes every man's
flesh put space on;and his mind take off time

and so we turn to poetry.

At the end of my preceding nonlecture, I read you five poems
celebrating spring. Tonight I shall try to read you five poems in
celebration of love. The first and second of these poems, by
Dante and by Shakespeare, are sonnets (for me the greatest
sonnets which exist). How anyone could say anything about the
third poem, a lyric by Robert Burns, I don't know. The fourth
poem—appropriately enough a big and long one—is called To
His Mistris Going To Bed; and John Donne wrote it. Finally
comes my favorite love poem: Under Der Linden, by the early
German poet Walther von der Vogelweide.

Tanto gentile e tanto onesta pare
   La donna mia, quand' ella altrui saluta,
   Ch' ogne lingua deven tremando muta,
   E li occhi no l' ardiscon di guardare.

Ella si va, sentendosi laudare,
   Benignamente d'umiltà vestuta;
   E par che sia una cosa venuta
   Da cielo in terra a mirácol mostrare.

Móstrasi si piacente a chi la mira,
   Che dà per li occhi una dolcezza al core,
   Ch' ntender no la può chi no la prova.

E par che della sua labbia si mova
   Un spirito soave pien d'amore,
   Che va dicendo all' anima: sospira.

Let me not to the marriage of true mindes
Admit impediments. Love is not love
Which alters when it alteration findes,
Or bends with the remover to remove.
O no, it is an ever fixed marke
That looks on tempests and is never shaken;
It is the star to every wandring barke,
Whose worth's unknowne, although his hight be taken.
Love's not Times foole, though rosie lips and cheeks
Within his bending sickles compasse come,
Love alters not with his breefe houres and weekes,
But beares it out even to the edge of doome:
    If this be error and upon me proved,
    I never writ, nor no man ever loved.

O my luve is like a red, red rose,
    That's newly sprung in June;
O my luve is like the melodie,
    That's sweetly played in tune.

As fair art thou, my bonie lass,
    So deep in luve am I;
And I will luve thee still, my dear,
    Till a' the seas gang dry.

Till a' the seas gang dry, my dear,
    And the rocks melt wi' the sun;
And I will luve thee still, my dear,
    While the sands o' life shall run.

And fare-thee-weel, my only luve!
    And fare-thee-weel a while!
And I will come again, my luve,
    Though it were ten thousand mile.

Come, Madam, come, all rest my powers defie,
Until I labour, I in labour lie.
The foe oft-times having the foe in sight,
Is tir'd with standing though he never fight.
Off with that girdle, like heavens Zone glittering,
But a far fairer world incompassing.
Unpin that spangled breastplate which you wear,
That th' eyes of busie fooles may be stopt there.
Unlace your self, for that harmonious chyme,
Tells me from you, that now it is bed time.
Off with that happy busk, which I envie,
That still can be, and still can stand so nigh.
Your gown going off, such beauteous state reveals,
As when from flowry meads th' hills shadow steales.
Off with that wyerie Coronet and shew
The haiery Diademe which on you doth grow:
Now off with those shooes, and then safely tread
In this loves hallow'd temple, this soft bed.
In such white robes, heavens Angels us'd to be
Receaved by men; Thou Angel bringst with thee
A heaven like Mahomets Paradise; and though
Ill spirits walk in white, we easly know
By this these Angels from an evil sprite,
Those set our hairs, but these our flesh upright.
    Licence my roaving hands, and let them go,
Before, behind, between, above, below.
O my America! my new-found-land,
My kingdome, safliest when with one man man'd,
My Myne of precious stones, my Emperie,
How blest am I in this discovering thee!
To enter in these bonds, is to be free;
Then where my hand is set, my seal shall be.
    Full nakedness! All joyes are due to thee,
As souls unbodied, bodies uncloth'd must be
To taste whole joyes. Gemes which you women use
Are like Atlanta's balls, cast in mens views,
That when a fools eye lighteth on a Gem,
His earthly soul may covet theirs, not them.
Like pictures, or like books gay coverings made
For lay-men, are all women thus array'd;
Themselves are mystick books, which only wee

(Whom their imputed grace will dignifie)
Must see reveal'd. Then since that I may know;
As liberally, as to a Midwife, shew
Thy self: cast all, yea, this white lynnen hence,
There is no pennance due to innocence.
    To teach thee, I am naked first; why then
What needst thou have more covering than a man.

Under der linden
an der heide,
dâ unser zweier bette was,
dâ mugt ir vinden
schône beide
gebrochen bluomen unde gras.
vor dem walde in einem tal,
tandaradei,
   schône sanc diu nahtegal.

Ich kam gegangen
zuo der ouwe:
dô was min friedel komen ê.
dâ wart ich enpfangen
hêre frouwe,
daz ich bin sælic iemer mê.
kuster mich? wol tûsentstunt:
tandaradei,
   seht wie rôt mir ist der munt.

Dô het er gemachet
alsô rîche
von bluomen eine bettestat.
des wirt noch gelachet
inneclîche,
kumt iemen an daz selbe pfat.
bî den rôsen er wol mac,
tandaradei,
   merken wâ mirz houbet lac.

Daz er bî mir læge,
wessez iemen
(nu enwelle got!), sô schamt ich mich.
wes er mit mir pflæge,
niemer niemen
bevinde daz, wan er unt ich,
und ein kleinez vogellîn:
tandaradei,
   daz mac wol getriuwe sîn.

i   &

you & is

NONLECTURE FOUR

Now comes, from my point of view, the excitement; and from yours, in all likelihood, the boredom—egocentrically supposing the boredom didn't come long ago. For I herewith assume (if possible even more egocentrically) that when we last met, or didn't meet, a certain longlost personage became EECummings: thereby reducing the aesthetic selfportrait of one whole half of this not divisible ignoramus to an exploration of his stance as a writer.

Writing, I feel, is an art; and artists, I feel, are human beings. As a human being stands, so a human being is: not that some human beings aren't acrobats, while others—but why anticipate Him and Santa Claus? Suffice it to say that the present non-poetical period will consist of nothing but sentences, essays, and parts of essays, all of which express a standing human being. I shall take these expressions chronologically; stating when they were published and how, but letting you draw your own (if any) conclusions. Over- and under-standing will make their appearance later: during the next thirty minutes, a particular human being will merely stand for thirty years.

1922—from my first published book, The Enormous Room

There are certain things in which one is unable to believe for the simple reason that he never ceases to feel them. Things of this sort— things which are always inside of us and in fact are us and which consequently will not be pushed off or away where we can begin thinking about them—are no longer things;they,and the us which they are,equals A Verb;an IS.

1926—from the foreword to a book of poems called Is 5

On the assumption that my technique is either complicated or original or both,the publishers have politely requested me to write an introduction to this book.

At least my theory of technique,if I have one,is very far from original;nor is it complicated. I can express it in fifteen words,by quoting The Eternal Question And Immortal Answer of burlesk,viz. "Would you hit a woman with a child?—No,I'd hit her with a brick." Like the burlesk comedian,I am abnormally fond of that precision which creates movement.

If a poet is anybody,he is somebody to whom things made matter very little—somebody who is obsessed by Making . . .

Ineluctable preoccupation with The Verb gives a poet one priceless advantage:whereas nonmakers must content themselves with the merely undeniable fact that two times two is four,he rejoices in an irresistible truth(to be found,in abbreviated costume, upon the title page of the present volume)

1927—An Imaginary Dialogue Between An Author And A Public, printed on the book-jacket of my first play

Author: Well?
Public: What is Him about?
Author: Why ask me? Did I or didn't I make the play?
Public: But surely you know what you're making—
Author: Beg pardon,Mr. Public;I surely make what I'm knowing.
Public: So far as I'm concerned,my very dear sir,nonsense isn't
         everything in life.
Author: And so far as you're concerned "life" is a verb of two
         voices—active,to do,and passive,to dream. Others believe
         doing to be only a kind of dreaming. Still others have
         discovered (in a mirror surrounded with mirrors),some-
         thing harder than silence but softer than falling;the third
         voice of "life",which believes itself and which cannot mean
         because it is.
Public: Bravo,but are such persons good for anything in particular?
Author: They are good for nothing but walking upright in the
         cordial revelation of the fatal reflexive.
Public: And your play is all about one of these persons,Mr. Author?
Author: Perhaps. But(let me tell you a secret)I rather hope my play
         is one of these persons.

1933—from my Soviet Russian diary, EIMI

Not to completely feel is thinking . . .

to grow is a fate.

People may dare to live,people may be taught or may teach themselves death;noone can learn growing. Noone can dare to grow. Growing equals that any reason or motive or unreason becomes every other unreason or reason or motive. Here exists no sign,no path,no distance,and no time . . . Drunk and becauseless(talking about a cyclone,telling how at last with the disappearance even of impossibility himself found actually himself and suddenly becoming the cyclone;not perishing and not surviving;Being)the poet Hart Crane was able to invent growth's likeness.

1934—from an introduction written for the Modern Library edition of The Enormous Room

When this book wrote itself,I was observing a negligible portion of something incredibly more distant than any sun;something more unimaginably huge than the most prodigious of all universes—
Namely?
The Individual.

Russia,I felt,was more deadly than war:when nationalists hate,they hate by merely killing and maiming human beings;when internationalists hate,they hate by categorying and pigeonholing human beings.

Eimi is the individual again;a more complex individual,a more enormous room.

1938—from an introduction written for my miscalled Collected Poems; thrice miscalled, since three books of poems (entitled 50 Poems, One Times One, and XAIPE) have already followed it

Take the matter of being born. What does being born mean to mostpeople? Catastrophe unmitigated. Social revolution . . . Mostpeople fancy a guaranteed birthproof safetysuit of nondestructible selflessness. If mostpeople were to be born twice they'd improbably call it dying—

you and I are not snobs. We can never be born enough. We are human beings;for whom birth is a supremely welcome mystery,the mystery of growing:the mystery which happens only and whenever we are faithful to ourselves . . . Life,for eternal us,is now . . .

What their most synthetic not to mention transparent majesty, mrsandmr collective foetus, would improbably call a ghost is walking . . . He is a healthily complex, a naturally homogeneous, citizen of immortality . . . He is a little more than everything,he is democracy;he is alive: he is ourselves.

. . . Nothing believed or doubted . . .

Always the beautiful answer who asks a more beautiful question

Here let me, momentarily interrupting my egocentric self, read you a pitying and terrible passage from the New Testament; on which our next selection (one of a pair of essays concerning Ezra Pound) is based. Most of you are no doubt acquainted with this more than most famous manifestation of whatever I can only call feeling—as against unfeeling: alias knowing and believing and thinking—this masterpoem of human perception, whose seventh verse alone exterminates all conventional morality

Jesus went unto the mount of Olives.

And early in the morning he came again into the temple, and all the people came unto him; and he sat down, and taught them.

And the scribes and Pharisees brought unto him a woman taken in
    a
    dultery; and when they had set her in the midst,

They say unto him, Master, this woman was taken in adultery, in the very act.

Now Moses in the law commanded us, that such should be stoned: but what sayest thou?

This they said, tempting him, that they might have to accuse him. But Jesus stooped down, and with his finger wrote on the ground, as though he heard them not.

So when they continued asking him, he lifted up himself, and said unto them, He that is without sin among you, let him first cast a stone at her.

And again he stooped down, and wrote on the ground.

And they which heard it, being convicted by their own conscience, went out one by one, beginning at the eldest, even unto the last: and Jesus was left alone, and the woman standing in the midst.

When Jesus had lifted up himself, and saw none but the woman, he said unto her, Woman, where are those thine accusers? hath no man condemned thee?

She saith, No man, Lord. And Jesus said unto her, Neither do I condemn thee: go, and sin no more.

Follows my essay—Anno Domini 1940—written at the request of Miss Frances Steloff, and published in her Gotham Book Mart catalogue entitled We Moderns

John,viii,7.
So now let us talk about something else. This is a free country because compulsory education. This is a free country because nobody has to eat. This is a free country because not any other country was is or ever will be free. So now you know and knowledge is power.

An interesting fact when you come right down to it is that simple people like complex things. But what amounts to an extraordinary coincidence is mediocre people liking firstrate things. The explanation can't be because complex things are simple. It must be because mediocre people are firstrate.

So now let us pull the wool over each other's toes and go to Hell. John,viii,7.

144—an essay prefacing the catalogue of an exhibition of my
paintings at the American British Art Center, New York City;
but whose subject isn't the art of painting and is Art Herself. In
this essay, four words—"good," "bad," "war," "peace"—are
surrounded by quotationmarks whenever they occur

Simple people,people who don't exist,prefer things which don't
exist,simple things.

"Good" and "bad" are simple things. You bomb me = "bad."
I bomb you = "good." Simple people(who,incidentally,run this
socalled world)know this(they know everything)whereas complex
people—people who feel something—are very,very ignorant and
really don't know anything.

Nothing,for simple knowing people,is more dangerous than
ignorance. Why?

Because to feel something is to be alive.

"War" and "peace" are not dangerous or alive:far from it.
"Peace" is the inefficiency of science. "War" is the science of
inefficiency. And science is knowing and knowing is measuring.

Ignorant people really must be educated;that is,they must be
made to stop feeling something,and compelled to begin knowing or
measuring everything. Then(then only)they won't threaten the
very nonexistence of what all simple people call civilization.

Very luckily for you and me,the uncivilized sun mysteriously
shines on "good" and "bad" alike. He is an artist.

Art is a mystery.

A mystery is something immeasurable.

In so far as every child and woman and man may be immeasurable,art is the mystery of every man and woman and child. In so
far as a human being is an artist,skies and mountains and oceans
and thunderbolts and butterflies are immeasurable;and art is every
mystery of nature. Nothing measurable can be alive;nothing which
is not alive can be art;nothing which cannot be art is true:and
everything untrue doesn't matter a very good God damn . . .

item:it is my complex hope that the pictures here exhibited
are neither "good" nor "bad",neither peacelike nor warful—that
(on the contrary)they are living.

68

1945—a contribution to Charles Norman's "symposium" (which sold out one issue of the shortlived newspaper PM) concerning this selfstyled world's greatest and most generous literary figure: who had just arrived at our nation's capitol, attired in half a GI uniform and ready to be hanged as a traitor by the only country which ever made even a pretense of fighting for freedom of speech

Re Ezra Pound—poetry happens to be an art;and artists happen to be human beings.

An artist doesn't live in some geographical abstraction,superimposed on a part of this beautiful earth by the nonimagination of unanimals and dedicated to the proposition that massacre is a social virtue because murder is an individual vice. Nor does an artist live in some soi-disant world,nor does he live in some socalled universe,nor does he live in any number of "worlds" or in any number of "universes". As for a few trifling delusions like the "past" and "present" and "future" of quote mankind unquote,they may be big enough for a couple of billion supermechanized submorons but they're much too small for one human being.

Every artist's strictly illimitable country is himself.

An artist who plays that country false has committed suicide; and even a good lawyer cannot kill the dead. But a human being who's true to himself—whoever himself may be—is immortal;and all the atomic bombs of all the antiartists in spacetime will never civilize immortality.

Also 1945—from an essay contributed to Oscar Williams' anthology called The War Poets

when you confuse art with propaganda,you confuse an act of God with something which can be turned on and off like the hot water faucet. If "God" means nothing to you(or less than noth cheerfully substitute one of your own favorite words,"fre

You confuse freedom—the only freedom—with absolute tyranny . . .
all over this socalled world,hundreds of millions of servile and
insolent inhuman unbeings are busily rolling and unrolling in the
enlightenment of propaganda. So what? There are still a few erect
human beings in the socalled world. Proudly and humbly,I say to
these human beings:

"O my fellow citizens,many an honest man believes a lie. Though
you are as honest as the day,fear and hate the liar. Fear and hate
him when he should be feared and hated:now. Fear and hate him
where he should be feared and hated:in yourselves.

"Do not hate and fear the artist in yourselves,my fellow citizens.
Honour him and love him. Love him truly—do not try to possess
him. Trust him as nobly as you trust tomorrow.

"Only the artist in yourselves is more truthful than the night."

1951—from an essay entitled Jottings, published in Wake magazine

equality is what does not exist among equals
most people are perfectly afraid of silence
great men burn bridges before they come to them
the pigpen is mightier than the sword
when Americans stop being themselves they start behaving each other
false is alike. False teeth
private property began the instant somebody had a mind of his own
a poet is a penguin—his wings are to swim with
people who live in steel houses should pull down the lightning
enter labor,with an itching heart and a palm of gold;leading(by
    the nose)humanity,in a unionsuit
a chain is no weaker than its missing link
hatred bounces
sleep is the mother of courage
an intelligent person fights for lost causes,realizing that others are
    merely effects
think twice before you think
knowledge is a polite word for dead but not buried imagination

Here endeth the fourth lesson—or, speaking precisely, my fourth lesson; since it's I who (thanks to you) am learning who I am. Let me now mercifully conclude our egocentric séance by reading, from that miraculous labour of love which is Francis James Child's English And Scottish Ballads, one great tragic and one great comic anonymity: one pitying and one terrible warning against inhuman unfeeling.

"Quhy dois zour brand sae drop w' bluid,
        Edward, Edward?
Quhy dois zour brand sae drop wi' bluid,
        And quhy sae sad gang zee O?"
"O I hae killed my hauke sae guid,
        Mither, mither:
O I hae killed my hauke sae guid,
        And I had nae mair bot hee O."

"Zour haukis bluid was nevir sae reid,
        Edward, Edward:
Zour haukis bluid was nevir sae reid,
        My deir son I tell thee O."
"O I hae killed my reid-roan steid,
        Mither, mither:
O I hae killed my reid-roan steid,
        That erst was sae fair and free O."

"Zour steid was auld, and ze hae gat mair,
        Edward, Edward:
Zour steid was auld, and ze hae gat mair,
        Sum other dule ze drie O."
"O I hae killed my fadir deir,
        Mither, mither:
O I hae killed my fadir deir,
        Alas! and wae is mee O!

"And quhatten penance wul ze drie, for that,
        Edward, Edward?
And quhatten penance will ze drie for that?
        My deir son, now tell me O."
"Ile set my feit in zonder boat,
        Mither, mither:
Ile set my feit in zonder boat,
        And Ile fare ovir the sea O."

"And quhat wul ze doe wi' zour towirs and zour ha',
        Edward, Edward?
And quhat wul ze doe wi' zour towirs and zour ha',
        That were sae fair to see O?"

"Ile let thame stand til they doun fa',
                    Mither, mither:
Ile let thame stand til they doun fa',
        For here nevir mair maun I bee O."

And quhat wul ze leive to zour bairns and zour wife,
                    Edward, Edward?
And quhat wul ze leive to zour bairns and zour wife,
        Quhan ze gang ovir the sea O?"
"The warldis room, late them beg throw life,
                    Mither, mither:
The warldis room, late them beg throw life,
        For thame nevir mair wul I see O."

"And quhat wul ze leive to zour ain mither deir,
                    Edward, Edward?
And quhat wul ze leive to zour ain mither deir?
        My deir son, now tell me O."
"The curse of hell frae me sall ze beir,
                    Mither, mither:
The curse of hell frae me sall ze beir,
        Sic counseils ze gave to me O."

An ancient story Ile tell you anon
Of a notable prince, that was called King John;
And he ruled England with maine and with might,
For he did great wrong, and maintein'd little right.

And Ile tell you a story, a story so merrye,
Concerning the Abbott of Canterburye;
How for his house-keeping and high renowne,
They rode poste for him to fair London towne.

An hundred men, the king did heare say,
The abbot kept in his house every day;
And fifty golde chaines, without any doubt,
In velvet coates waited the abbot about.

"How now, father abbot, I heare it of thee,
Thou keepest a farre better house than mee;
And for thy house-keeping and high renowne,
I feare thou work'st treason against my crown."

"My liege," quo' the abbot, "I would it were knowne
I never spend nothing, but what is my owne;
And I trust your grace will doe me no deere,
For spending of my owne true-gotten geere."

"Yes, yes, father abbot, thy fault it is highe,
And now for the same thou needest must dye;
For except thou canst answer me questions three,
Thy head shall be smitten from thy bodie.

"And first," quo' the king, "when I'm in this stead,
With my crowne of gold so faire on my head,
Among all my liege-men so noble of birthe,
Thou must tell me to one penny what I am worthe.

Secondlye, tell me, without any doubt,
How soone I may ride the whole world about;
And at the third question thou must not shrink,
But tell me here truly what I do think."

"O these are hard questions for my shallow witt,
Nor I cannot answer your grace as yet:
But if you will give me but three weekes space,
Ile do my endeavour to answer your grace."

"Now three weeks space to thee will I give,
And that is the longest time thou hast to live;
For if thou dost not answer my questions three,
Thy lands and thy livings are forfeit to mee."

Away rode the abbot all sad at that word,
And he rode to Cambridge, and Oxenford;
But never a doctor there was so wise,
That could with his learning an answer devise.

Then home rode the abbot of comfort so cold.
And he mett his shepheard a going to fold:
"How now, my lord abbot, you are welcome home;
What newes do you bring us from good King John?"

"Sad newes, sad newes, shepheard, I must give,
That I have but three days more to live;
For if I do not answer him questions three,
My head will be smitten from my bodie.

"The first is to tell him there in that stead,
With his crowne of golde so fair on his head,
Among all his liege-men so noble of birth,
To within one penny of what he is worth.

"The seconde, to tell him, without any doubt,
How soone he may ride this whole world about;
And at the third question I must not shrinke,
But tell him there truly what he does thinke."

"Now cheare up, sire abbot, did you never hear yet,
That a fool may learne a wise man witt?
Lend me horse, and serving men, and your apparel,
And Ile ride to London to answere your quarrel.

"Nay frowne not, if it hath bin told unto mee,
I am like your lordship, as ever may bee;
And if you will but lend me your gowne,
There is none shall knowe us at fair London towne."

"Now horses and serving-men thou shalt have,
With sumptuous array most gallant and brave,
With crosier, and miter, and rochet, and cope,
Fit to appear 'fore our fader the pope."

"Now, welcome, sire abbot," the king he did say,
"'Tis well thou'rt come back to keepe thy day:
For and if thou canst answer my questions three,
Thy life and thy living both saved shall bee.

"And first, when thou seest me here in this stead,
With my crowne of golde so fair on my head,
Among all my liege-men so noble of birthe,
Tell me to one penny what I am worth."

"For thirty pence our Saviour was sold
Among the false Jewes, as I have been told:
And twenty-nine is the worth of thee,
For I thinke thou art one penny worser than hee."

The king he laughed, and swore by St. Bittel,
"I did not think I had been worth so littel!
—Now secondly tell me, without any doubt,
How soone I may ride this whole world about."

"You must rise with the sun, and ride with the same
Until the next morning he riseth againe;
And then your grace need not make any doubt
But in twenty-four hours you'll ride it about."

The king he laughed, and swore by St. Jone,
"I did not think it could be gone so soone;
—Now from the third question thou must not shrinke,
But tell me here truly what I do thinke."

"Yea, that shall I do, and make your grace merry;
You thinke I'm the abbot of Canterbury;
But I'm his poor shepheard, as plain you may see,
That am come to beg pardon for him and for mee."

The king he laughed, and swore by the masse,
"Ile make thee lord abbot this day in his place!"
"Now naye, my liege, be not in such speede,
For alacke I can neither write ne reade."

"Four nobles a week, then I will give thee,
For this merry jest thou has showne unto mee;
And tell the old abbot when thou comest home,
Thou hast brought him a pardon from good King John."

i &

now & him

NONLECTURE FIVE

Two weeks hence (in the course of my sixth and last nonlecture) I should greatly enjoy testing, by one particular individual's purely personal values, those complementary aspects of a soi-disant world known as communism and capitalism. Therefore it would more than delight me if this evening all abstractions which we have so far encountered should take unto themselves life; thus creating those very values. Since the mere abstractions —however various—concern themselves with being and with growing, my hope is that tonight you and I may actually feel what growing and being are. Perhaps through a single brief but significant passage from a quarter-of-a-century-young play, plus a few selections from three recently published books of poems, just this miracle may happen. Quite parenthetically, I doubt if many of you have ever met the ten sonnets which I shall later read; and am sure that most of you have neither perused nor beheld a drama whose loving nonhero and lovely heroine are called Him and Me; whose possibly principal protagonist impersonates (on various occasions) nine other people; whose so-to-speak-chorus consists of a trio of Weird Sisters; and whose twenty-one scenes revolve the distinction between time and eternity, measurable when and illimitable now. Also parenthetically—after the passage I am about to read you had written itself, I drew a picture of it; and this picture adorned certain sacrosanct copies of the first edition of a play called Him.

HIM: Damn everything but the circus! (*To himself*) And here am I, patiently squeezing fourdimensional ideas into a twodimensional stage, when all of me that's anyone or anything is in the top of a circustent . . . (*A pause*)
ME: I didn't imagine you were leading a double life—and right under my nose, too.
HIM (*Unhearing, proceeds contemptuously*): The average "painter" "sculptor" "poet" "composer" "playwright" is a person who cannot leap through a hoop from the back of a galloping horse, make people laugh with a clown's mouth, orchestrate twenty lions.

ME: Indeed.

HIM (*To her*): But imagine a human being who balances three chairs, one on top of another, on a wire, eighty feet in air with no net underneath, and then climbs into the top chair, sits down, and begins to swing . . .

ME (*Shudders*): I'm glad I never saw that—makes me dizzy just to think of it.

HIM (*Quietly*): I never saw that either.

ME: Because nobody can do it.

HIM: Because I am that. But in another way, it's all I ever see.

ME: What is?

HIM (*Pacing up and down*): This: I feel only one thing, I have only one conviction; it sits on three chairs in Heaven. Sometimes I look at it, with terror; it is such a perfect acrobat! The three chairs are three facts—it will quickly kick them out from under itself and will stand on air; and in that moment (because everyone will be disappointed) everyone will applaud. Meanwhile, some thousands of miles over everyone's head, over a billion empty faces, it rocks carefully and smilingly on three things, on three facts, on: I am an Artist, I am a Man, I am a Failure—it rocks and it swings and it smiles and it does not collapse tumble or die because it pays no attention to anything except itself. (*Passionately*) I feel, I am aware—every minute, every instant, I watch this trick, I am this trick, I sway—selfish and smiling and careful—above all the people. (*To himself*) And always I am repeating a simple and dark and little formula . . . always myself mutters and remutters a trivial colourless microscopic idiom—I breathe, and I swing; and I whisper: "An artist, a man, a failure, MUST PROCEED."

ME (*Timidly, after a short pause*): This thing or person who is you, who does not pay any attention to anyone else, it will stand on air?

HIM: On air. Above the faces, lives, screams—suddenly. Easily: alone.

ME: How about the chairs?

HIM: The chairs will all fall by themselves down from the wire and be caught by anybody, by nobody; by somebody whom I don't see and who doesn't see me: perhaps by everybody.

ME: Maybe yourself—you, away up ever so high—will hear me applaud?

HIM (*Looking straight at her, smiles seriously*): I shall see your eyes. I shall hear your heart move.

ME: Because I shall not be disappointed, like the others.

Speaking for myself—this fragment of dialogue renders vivid a whole bevy of abstractions; among which I recognize immediately three mysteries: love, art, and selftranscendence or growing. Since our nonhero calls himself an artist, let us take him at his word; and give art the emphasis. Our artist (whose agonizing privilege is to feel himself, except at timeless moments, a would-be artist) here vizualizes this anguished himself as a circus acrobat; performing an impossible feat above a vast multitude of un-understandingly enthralled spectators. Aside from their failure to understand him, nothing (doubtless) could be a greater violation of fact—yet precisely by this violation he tells us something far beyond either fact or fiction; a strictly unmitigated personal truth: namely, how he feels. And how does he feel? As someone absolutely and totally alone from the beginning of the world: a solitary individual who "sits on three chairs in heaven"; separated from everybody else by an-at-any-moment-fatal chasm which symbolizes his individuality, and without which he would cease to exist at all. No mere temporally measurable nonmystery can have any slightest meaning for this illimitable aloneness—yet (and here is perhaps the essence of the mystery) this incarnation of isolation is also a lover; so deeply identified with one particular member of the multitude beneath him that, if selftranscendence actually occurs, and someone who has died in time is reborn in timelessness, he will feel his beloved's heart leap with joy. On the one hand a complete fanatic, dedicated to values beyond life and death, he is on the other hand a profoundly alive and supremely human being.

Please note, and note well, the "trivial colourless microscopic idiom" which (in his birth-agony) our nonhero "mutters and remutters"—"an artist, a man, a failure, MUST PROCEED." Proceed: not succeed. With success, as any world or unworld comprehends it, he has essentially nothing to do. If it should come, well and good: but what makes him climb to the top of the tent emphatically isn't "a billion empty faces." Even success in his own terms cannot concern him otherwise than as a stimulus to further, and a challenge to more unimaginable, self-discovering—"The chairs will all fall by themselves down from the wire"; and who catches or who doesn't catch them is none of his immortal business. One thing, however, does always concern this individual: fidelity to himself. No simple (if abstruse) system of measurable soi-disant facts, which anybody can think and believe and know—or, when another system becomes popular; and the erstwhile facts become fictions—can unthink and unbelieve and unknow—has power over a complex truth which he, and he alone, can feel.

Let us make no mistake: Him is himself and nobody else—not even Me. But supposing Him to exemplify that mythical entity "the artist," we should go hugely astray in assuming that art was the only selftranscendence. Art is a mystery; all mysteries have their source in a mystery-of-mysteries who is love: and if lovers may reach eternity directly through love herself, their mystery remains essentially that of the loving artist whose way must lie through his art, and of the loving worshipper whose aim is oneness with his god. From another point of view, every human being is in and of himself or herself illimitable; but the essence of his or of her illimitability is precisely its uniqueness— nor could all poetry (past present and future) begin to indicate the varieties of selfhood; and consequently of selftranscendence. Luckily for the poems which I shall read, they have no such ambition. All they hope to do is to suggest that particular awareness without which no human spirit ever dreams of rising from such unmysteries as thinking and believing and knowing.

And so, having said far too much about a small prose passage, I turn with good courage to a few brief poems; letting them (at any rate) sing for themselves.

when serpents bargain for the right to squirm
and the sun strikes to gain a living wage—
when thorns regard their roses with alarm
and rainbows are insured against old age

when every thrush may sing no new moon in
if all screech-owls have not okayed his voice
—and any wave signs on the dotted line
or else an ocean is compelled to close

when the oak begs permission of the birch
to make an acorn—valleys accuse their
mountains of having altitude—and march
denounces april as a saboteur

then we'll believe in that incredible
unanimal mankind(and not until)

why must itself up every of a park

anus stick some quote statue unquote to
prove that a hero equals any jerk
who was afraid to dare to answer "no"?

quote citizens unquote might otherwise
forget(to err is human;to forgive
divine)that if the quote state unquote says
"kill" killing is an act of christian love.

"Nothing" in 1944 A D

"can stand against the argument of mil
itary necessity"(generalissimo e)
and echo answers "there is no appeal

from reason"(freud)—you pays your money and
you doesn't take your choice.   Aint freedom grand

all ignorance toboggans into know
and trudges up to ignorance again:
but winter's not forever,even snow
melts;and if spring should spoil the game,what then?

all history's a winter sport or three:
but were it five,i'd still insist that all
history's too small for even me;
for me and you,exceedingly too small.

Swoop(shrill collective myth)into thy grave
merely to toil the scale to shrillerness
per every madge and mabel dick and dave
—tomorrow is our permanent address

and there they'll scarcely find us(if they do,
we'll move away still further:into now

life is more true than reason will deceive
(more secret or than madness did reveal)
deeper is life than lose:higher than have
—but beauty is more each than living's all

multiplied by infinity sans if
the mightiest meditations of mankind
cancelled are by one merely opening leaf
(beyond whose nearness there is no beyond)

or does some littler bird than eyes can learn
look up to silence and completely sing?
futures are obsolete;pasts are unborn
(here less than nothing's more than everything)

death,as men call him,ends what they call men
—but beauty is more now than dying's when

no man,if men are gods;but if gods must
be men,the sometimes only man is this
(most common,for each anguish is his grief;
and,for his joy is more than joy,most rare)

a fiend,if fiends speak truth;if angels burn

by their own generous completely light,
an angel;or(as various worlds he'll spurn
rather than fail immeasurable fate)
coward,clown,traitor,idiot,dreamer,beast—

such was a poet and shall be and is

—who'll solve the depths of horror to defend
a sunbeam's architecture with his life:
and carve immortal jungles of despair
to hold a mountain's heartbeat in his hand

hate blows a bubble of despair into
hugeness world system universe and bang
—fear buries a tomorrow under woe
and up comes yesterday most green and young

pleasure and pain are merely surfaces
(one itself showing,itself hiding one)
life's only and true value neither is
love makes the little thickness of the coin

comes here a man would have from madame death
neverless now and without winter spring?
she'll spin that spirit her own fingers with
and give him nothing(if he should not sing)

how much more than enough for both of us
darling. And if I sing you are my voice

one's not half two. It's two are halves of one:
which halves reintegrating,shall occur
no death or any quantity;but than
all numerable mosts the actual more

minds ignorant of stern miraculous
this every truth—beware of heartless them
(given the scalpel,they dissect a kiss;
or,sold the reason,they undream a dream)

one is the song which fiends and angels sing:
all murdering lies by mortals told make two.
Let liars wilt,repaying life they're loaned;
we(by a gift called dying born)must grow

deep in dark least ourselves remembering
love only rides his year.
                              All lose,whole find

if(touched by love's own secret)we,like homing
through welcoming sweet miracles of air
(and joyfully all truths of wing resuming)
selves,into infinite tomorrow steer

—souls under whom flow(mountain valley forest)
a million wheres which never may become
one(wholly strange;familiar wholly)dearest
more than reality of more than dream—

how should contented fools of fact envision
the mystery of freedom?yet,among
their loud exactitudes of imprecision,
you'll(silently alighting)and i'll sing

while at us very deafly a most stares
colossal hoax of clocks and calendars

i thank You God for most this amazing
day:for the leaping greenly spirits of trees
and a blue true dream of sky;and for everything
which is natural which is infinite which is yes

(i who have died am alive again today,
and this is the sun's birthday;this is the birth
day of life and of love and wings:and of the gay
great happening illimitably earth)

how should tasting touching hearing seeing
breathing any—lifted from the no
of all nothing—human merely being
doubt unimaginable You?

(now the ears of my ears awake and
now the eyes of my eyes are opened)

true lovers in each happening of their hearts
live longer than all which and every who;
despite what fear denies,what hope asserts,
what falsest both disprove by proving true

(all doubts,all certainties,as villains strive
and heroes through the mere mind's poor pretend
—grim comics of duration:only love
immortally occurs beyond the mind)

such a forever is love's any now
and her each here is such an everywhere,
even more true would truest lovers grow
if out of midnight dropped more suns than are

(yes;and if time should ask into his was
all shall,their eyes would never miss a yes)

Here my fifth lesson ends—a lesson based on selfhood and selftranscendence. By way of celebrating its ending, this ignorant
human being would like to share with you what are (for him, at
least) the supreme expressions of those values in all literature.
His sharing will involve a large part of the final scene of Shakespeare's Antony and Cleopatra, and the opening lines of the
thirty-third canto of Dante's Paradise. Let me only add that I
can imagine nothing more difficult to attempt, and nothing
better worth attempting.

Dolabella. Madam, as thereto sworn by your command,
Which my love makes religion to obey,
I tell you this: Cæsar through Syria
Intends his journey; and within three days
You with your children will he send before.
Make your best use of this; I have perform'd
Your pleasure and my promise.
 Cleopatra.   Dolabella,
I shall remain your debtor.
 Dol.   I your servant.
Adieu, good queen; I must attend on Cæsar.
 Cleo. Farewell, and thanks.

            [*Exit* Dolabella
       Now, Iras, what think'st thou?
Thou, an Egyptian puppet, shall be shown
In Rome, as well as I; mechanic slaves
With greasy aprons, rules and hammers, shall
Uplift us to the view; in their thick breaths,
Rank of gross diet, shall we be enclouded,
And forc'd to drink their vapour.
 Iras.   The gods forbid!
 Cleo. Nay, 'tis most certain, Iras. Saucy lictors
Will catch at us, like strumpets, and scald rimers
Ballad us out o' tune; the quick comedians
Extemporally will stage us, and present
Our Alexandrian revels. Antony
Shall be brought drunken forth, and I shall see
Some squeaking Cleopatra boy my greatness
I' the posture of a whore.
 Iras.   O, the good gods!
 Cleo. Nay, that's certain.
 Iras. I'll never see 't; for, I am sure my nails
Are stronger than mine eyes.
 Cleo.   Why, that's the way
To fool their preparation, and to conquer
Their most absurd intents.
     Re-enter Charmian.
       Now, Charmian,
Show me, my women, like a queen; go fetch
My best attires; I am again for Cydnus,

To meet Mark Antony. Sirrah Iras, go.
Now, noble Charmian, we'll dispatch indeed;
And, when thou hast done this chare, I'll give thee leave
To play till doomsday. Bring our crown and all.

[*Exit* IRAS. *A noise heard.*

Wherefore's this noise?

Enter one of the GUARD.

Guard.   Here is a rural fellow
That will not be denied your highness' presence:
He brings you figs.

Cleo. Let him come in. [*Exit Guard.*] What poor an instrument
May do a noble deed! he brings me liberty.
My resolution 's plac'd, and I have nothing
Of woman in me; now from head to foot
I am marble-constant, now the fleeting moon
No planet is of mine.

Re-enter Guard, *with* a Clown *bringing in a basket.*

Guard.   This is the man.

Cleo. Avoid, and leave him.   [*Exit Guard.*
Hast thou the pretty worm of Nilus there,
That kills and pains not?

Clo. Truly, I have him; but I would not be the party that
should desire you to touch him, for his biting is immortal; those that
do die of it do seldom or never recover.

Cleo. Remember'st thou any that have died on 't?

Clo. Very many, men and women too. I heard of one of them
no longer than yesterday; a very honest woman, but something
given to lie, as a woman should not do but in the way of honesty;
how she died of the biting of it, what pain she felt. Truly, she makes
a very good report o' the worm; but he that will believe all that
they say shall never be saved by half that they do. But this is most
fallible, the worm's an odd worm.

Cleo. Get thee hence; farewell.

Clo. I wish you all joy of the worm.

[*Sets down the basket.*

Cleo. Farewell.

Clo. You must think this, look you, that the worm will do
his kind.

Cleo. Ay, ay; farewell.

Clo. Look you, the worm is not to be trusted but in the keeping
of wise people; for indeed there is no goodness in the worm.

94

Cleo. Take thou no care, it shall be heeded.

Clo. Very good. Give it nothing, I pray you, for it is not worth the feeding.

Cleo. Will it eat me?

Clo. You must not think I am so simple but I know the devil himself will not eat a woman; I know that a woman is a dish for the gods, if the devil dress her not. But, truly, these same whoreson devils do the gods great harm in their women, for in every ten that they make, the devils mar five.

Cleo. Well, get thee gone; farewell.

Clo. Yes, forsooth; I wish you joy of the worm.   [*Exit.*

    Re-enter IRAS *with a robe, crown, etc.*

Cleo. Give me my robe, put on my crown; I have
Immortal longings in me; now no more
The juice of Egypt's grape shall moist this lip.
Yare, yare, good Iras; quick. Methinks I hear
Antony call; I see him rouse himself
To praise my noble act; I hear him mock
The luck of Cæsar, which the gods give men
To excuse their after wrath: husband, I come:
Now to that name my courage prove my title!
I am fire, and air; my other elements
I give to baser life. So; have you done?
Come then, and take the last warmth of my lips.
Farewell, kind Charmian; Iras, long farewell.

    [*Kisses them.* IRAS *falls and dies.*

Have I the aspic in my lips? Dost fall?
If thou and nature can so gently part,
The stroke of death is as a lover's pinch,
Which hurts, and is desir'd. Dost thou lie still?
If thus thou vanishest, thou tell'st the world
It is not worth leave-taking.

Char. Dissolve, thick cloud, and rain; that I may say
The gods themselves do weep.

Cleo.   This proves me base:
If she first meet the curled Antony,
He'll make demand of her, and spend that kiss
Which is my heaven to have. Come, thou mortal wretch,

    [*To the asp, which she applies to her breast.*

With thy sharp teeth this knot intrinsicate
Of life at once untie, poor venomous fool,

Be angry, and dispatch. O! couldst thou speak,
That I might hear thee call great Cæsar ass
Unpoliced.

    Char.   O eastern star!

    Cleo.   Peace, peace!
Dost thou not see my baby at my breast,
That sucks the nurse asleep?

Vergine Madre, figlia del tuo Figlio,
    umile ed alta più che creatura,
    termine fisso d'eterno consiglio,

tu se' colei che l' umana natura
    nobilitasti sì, che il suo Fattore
    non disdegnò di farsi sua fattura.

Nel ventre tuo si raccese l' amore,
    per lo cui caldo nell' eterna pace
    Così è germinato questo fiore.

Qui sei a noi meridiana face
    di caritate, e giuso intra i mortali,
    sei di speranza fontana vivace.

Donna, sei tanto grande e tanto vali,
    che qual vuol grazia ed a te non ricorre,
    Sua disïanza vuol volar senz' ali.

La tua benignità non pur soccorre
    a chi domanda, ma molte fiate
    liberamente al domandar precorre.

In te misericordia, in te pietate,
    in te magnificenza, in te s' aduna
    quantunque in creatura è di bontate.

i &

am & santa claus

NONLECTURE SIX

This evening I shall try to do four things—first, read you a single lengthy passage from a Soviet Russian diary—second, escort you through a five-scene morality play called Santa Claus—third, consider a question which asked itself at the beginning of nonlecture one—and finally, leave you in the company of two great human beings.

Since most of my auditors have neither visited Karl Marx's paradise nor encountered a vastly unpopular book entitled EIMI (which, by the by, is written in a style of its own) I shall take the liberty of describing just what happens during the next fifteen minutes. On Saturday, May thirtieth, nineteen hundred and thirty-one, in the desolate city of Moscow, I glimpse an apparently endless line of unimaginably uncouth figures (each a tovarich or comrade; a soi-disant citizen of the subhuman superstate USSR) moving imperceptibly toward, and disappearing into, the tomb of their human god Lenin; whose embalmed body supposedly lies somewhere within and below. I approach an officer of the nonlaw, looming near the tomb's entrance; and (mustering all my mendacity) tell him that I'm an American newspaperman: whereupon he salutingly shoves me in the very front of the line. As the line unmovingly moves, I enter the tomb; I descend; I view the human god Lenin; I ascend; I emerge—and then (breathing fresh air once more) I marvel: not so much at what I have, as at what I have not, seen.

Let me add that the Greek word $\epsilon i \mu i$ signifies am; that "comrade K" (for Kemminkz, a Russian version of Cummings) equals myself; and that "Arabian Nights" is myself's petname for Moscow's most marvellously magnificent church—or rather, once upon a time church; since the benevolent atheist government has turned it into an antireligious museum.

Here we adventure Am—

facefacefaceface
  hand-
       fin-
         claw
  foot-
     hoof
  (tovarich)
        es to number of numberlessness(un
-smiling)
with dirt's dirt dirty dirtier with others' dirt with dirt of themselves dirtiest waitstand dirtily never smile ,shufflebudge dirty pause-
halt
  Smilingless.
        Some from nowhere(faces of nothing)others out of
somewhere(somethingshaped hands)these knew ignorance(hugest feet
and believing)those were friendless(stooping in their deathskins)all—
  numberlessly
  —eachotherish
  facefacefaceface
  facefaceface
  faceface
  Face
    :all(of whom-which move-do-not-move numberlessly)Toward
the
    Tomb
        Crypt
           Shrine
Grave.
The grave.
Toward the(grave.
All toward the grave)of himself of herself(all toward the grave of
themselves)all toward the grave of Self.
Move(with dirt's dirt dirty)unmoving move un(some from nowhere)moving move unmoving(eachotherish)
  :face
Our-not-their
faceface;
Our-not-her
,facefaceface
Our-not-his
       —toward

Vladimir our life!Ulianov our sweetness!Lenin our hope!
all—
(hand-
        fin-
            claw
foot-
    hoof
tovarich)
                es:to number of numberlessness;un
-smiling
    all toward Un- moveunmove,all toward Our haltpause;all toward
All budgeshuffle:all toward Toward standwait. Isn'tish.
    The dark human All warped(the Un-)toward and—facefaceface-
face—past Arabian Nights and disappearing . . . numberlessness;or
may possibly there exist an invisible,a final,face;moveunmovingly
which after several forevers will arrive to(hushed)look upon its
maker Lenin?
    "pahjahlstah"—voice?belonging to comrade K. Said to a most
tough cop. Beside shufflebudging end of beginninglessness,before the
Tomb of Tombs,standunstanding.
    (Voice?continues)I,American correspondent . . .
    (the toughest cop spun:upon all of and over smallest me staring
all 1 awful moment—salutes! And very gently shoves)let the skies
snow dolphins—nothing shall confound us now!(into smilelessly the
entering beginning of endlessness:
    —between these 2 exhausted its:a
    bearded,and a merely
unshaven)now who emotionlessly displace themselves. Obediently
and now we form a dumb me-sandwich. & now which,moves
    3 comrades move;comrade before me(comrade I)comrade behind
me . . . un- . . . and   move . . . and   un- . . . and   always(behind
comrade behind me)numb-erl-ess-ness
    (at either side of the Portal:rigidity. Armed soldier attentioning)
    —stink;warm poresbowels,millionary of man-the-unanimal
putresence. Floods up from dark. Suffocatingly envelopes 3 now
(unmovemoving past that attentioning twain each(& whose
eyelids moveunmove)other facing rigidities)comrades
    as when a man inhabits,for stars and moons,freely himself
(breathing always round air;living deeply the colour of darkness and
utterly enjoying the sound of the great sun;tasting very slowly a
proud silence of mountains;touched by,touching,what never to be

comprehended miracles;conversing with trees fearlessly and fire and
rain and all creatures and each strong faithful thing)as when the man
comes to a where tremulous with despair and a when luminous with
dissolution—into all fearfulness comes,out of omnipotence—as when he
enters a city(and solemnly his soul descends:every wish covers its
beauty in tomorrow)so I descended and so I disguised myself;so
(toward death's deification moving)I did not move

    bearded's cap slumps off. Mine. Beardless's

    . . . now,Stone;polished(Now)darklyness . . .

    —leftturning:

                Down

    (the old skull floating(the old ghost shuffling)just-in-front-of-me
in-stink-and-glimmer &

    from)whom,now:forth creeps,som(ething,timi)dly . . . a Feeling
tenta-

    cle cau,tiously &,which,softlytouchtry-ing fear,ful,ly how the
polished the slippery black,the—is it real?—(da)amazedly & with-
draws;diminishes;wilt

    -ing(rightturn)

                as we enter The Place,I look up:over(all)us a
polished slab reflecting upside(com(moveunmoving)rades)down.
Now;a. Pit:here . . . yes—sh!

    under a prismshaped transparency

    lying(tovarich-to-the-waist

    forcelessly shut rightclaw

    leftfin unshut limply

    & a small-not-intense head & a face-without-wrinkles & a
reddish beard).

    (1 appearing quickly uniform shoves our singleness into 2s)yanks
bearded to the inside pushes to the outside me . . . & as un(around
the(the prism)pit)movingly comrades the move

    (within a neckhigh wall

    in a groove which surrounds the prism)

    stands,at the prism's neuter pole,a human being (alive,silent) with
a real rifle:

    —comrades revolve. Wheel we. Now I am somehow(for a moment)
on the inside;alone—

    growls. Another soldier. Rightturning us. Who leave The Place
(whose walls irregularly are splotched with red frieze)leave the
dumb saccharine porebowel ripeness of stink . . . we climb &
climbing we

    're out.

Certainly it was not made of flesh. And I have seen so many wax-works which were actual(some ludicrous more horrible most both) so many images whose very unaliveness could liberate Is,invent Being(or what equally disdains life and unlife)—I have seen so very many better gods or stranger,many mightier deeper puppets;everywhere and elsewhere and perhaps in America and(for instance)in Coney Island . . .

So much (or so little) for one major aspect of the inhuman unworld: a fanatical religion of irreligion, conceived by sterile intellect and nurtured by omnipotent nonimagination. From this gruesome apotheosis of mediocrity in the name of perfectibility, this implacable salvation of all through the assassination of each, this reasoned enormity of spiritual suicide, I turn to a complementary—and if possible even more monstrous—phenomenon. That phenomenon is a spiritually impotent pseudocommunity enslaved by perpetual obscenities of mental concupiscence; an omnivorous social hypocrisy, vomiting vitalities of idealism while grovelling before the materialization of its own deathwish: a soi-disant free society, dedicated to immeasurable generosities of love; but dominated by a mere and colossal lust for knowing, which threatens not simply to erase all past and present and future human existence but to annihilate (in the name of liberty) Life Herself.

Here we begin my little allegory in blank verse; whose characters are Death, Santa Claus, Mob, Child, and Woman.

SCENE ONE

> (Death, strolling—he wears black tights on which the bones of his skeleton are vividly suggested by daubs of white paint; and his mask imitates crudely the face of a fleshless human skull. Enter, slowly and despondently, a prodigiously paunchy figure in faded red moth-eaten Santa Claus costume, with the familiar Santa Claus mask-face of a bewhiskered jolly old man)

Death.   Something wrong, brother?

Santa Claus.	Yes.
Death.	Sick?
Santa Claus.	Sick at heart.
Death.	What seems to be the trouble? Come—speak out.
Santa Claus.	I have so much to give; and nobody will take.
Death.	My problem is also one of distribution,
	only it happens to be the other way round.

Emanating friendliness, Death explains that he and Santa Claus are living in "a world so blurred that its inhabitants are one another"; "a world so false, so trivial, so unso" that "phantoms are solid by comparison." "This is a world of salesmanship" (he continues) and you are so unlucky as to be gifted with understanding; "the only thing which simply can't be sold." What you should do is to become a Scientist—"Or, in plain English, a knowledge-salesman"—since

> In this empty un-understanding world
> anyone can sell knowledge; everybody wants knowledge,
> and there's no price people won't pay to get it.

But (objects Santa Claus) it appears that "I have no knowledge . . . only understanding—"

Death.	Forget your understanding for a while,
	(*he plucks off Santa Claus' mask, revealing a young man's face*)
	and as for knowledge, why, don't let that worry you:
	(*he slips off his own mask, revealing a fleshless human skull,*
	and crams the skull mask over the young face of Santa Claus)
	once people hear the magic name of "Science"
	(*slipping the Santa Claus mask over his own skull face*)
	you can sell people anything—except understanding.
Santa Claus.	Yes?
Death.	Anything at all.
Santa Claus.	You mean, provided—
Death.	Provided nothing!

Santa Claus.	You don't mean to tell me
	I could sell people something which didn't exist?
Death.	Why not? You don't suppose people exist, do you?
Santa Claus.	Don't people exist?
Death.	People? —I'll say they don't!
	I wish to heaven they did exist; in that case
	I shouldn't be the skeleton I am.
	No—in this "Science" game, this "knowledge" racket,
	infinity's your limit; but remember:
	the less something exists, the more people want it.
Santa Claus.	I can't seem to think of anything which doesn't exist
	—perhaps you could help me.
Death.	How about a wheelmine?
Santa Claus.	A wheelmine?
Death.	Surely a wheelmine doesn't exist
	and never will, and never has existed.
Santa Claus.	A wheelmine . . . but that's perfectly fantastic!
Death.	Why say "fantastic" when you mean "Scientific"?
	—Well, I'll be strolling. So long, Mister Scientist!

Next we behold Santa Claus—now masked as Death and loudly proclaiming himself a Scientist—in the act of selling shares of wheelmine stock to a Mob; whose rampant skepticism rapidly turns to wild enthusiasm.

Santa Claus.	—Anybody else?
Voices.	Me! Me, too! Gimme!
Santa Claus.	—Just a moment. Friends,
	it never shall be said that Science favored
	or slighted anyone. Remember: Science
	is no mere individual. Individuals
	are, after all, nothing but human beings;
	and human beings are corruptible:
	for (as you doubtless know) to err is human.
	Think—only think! for untold centuries
	this earth was overrun by human beings!
	Think: it was not so many years ago
	that individuals could be found among us!
	O those dark ages! What a darkness, friends!

But now that hideous darkness turns to light;
the flame of Science blazes far and wide:
Science, impartial and omnipotent,
before whose superhuman radiance
all dark prescientific instincts vanish.
Think—only think! at last the monster, man,
is freed from his obscene humanity!
—While men were merely men, and nothing more,
what was equality? A word. A dream.
Men never could be equal—why? Because
equality's the attribute of supermen
like you, and you, and you, and you. And therefore
(superladies and supergentlemen)
when the impartial ear of Science hears
your superhuman voices crying "gimme,"
Science responds in Its omnipotence
"let there be enough wheelmine stock for all."

Voices.   Adda baby! Long live Science! Hooray for wheelmines!

As Scene Three opens, Santa Claus—in terror of his life—comes
running to Death: crying that there's been a terrible accident
in the wheelmine; and, as a consequence, the enthusiastic Mob
now wants to lynch him. Death, secretly delighted, pooh-poohs
the whole matter; and coolly assures his victim that a wheelmine is something perfectly nonexistent.

Santa Claus.   O, then tell me; tell me:
how can it maim, how can it mutilate;
how can it turn mere people into monsters:
answer me—how!

Death.   My friend, you've forgotten something:
namely, that people, like wheelmines, don't exist
—two negatives, you know, make an affirmative.
Now if I may be allowed to analyze—

Santa Claus.   Do you want to die?

Death.   I die? Ha-ha-ha-ha! How could Death die?

Santa Claus.   —Death?

Death.   Didn't you know?

Santa Claus.   I'm going mad. You: tell me,
              whatever you are, Death or the Devil, tell me:
              how can I prove I'm not to blame for the damage
              caused by an accident which never happened
              to people who are nonexistent?
     Death.   You can't.
Santa Claus. My God—but what am I going to do, then?
     Death.   Do?
              Why, my dear fellow, it looks to me as if
              you'd have to prove you don't exist yourself.
Santa Claus. But that's absurd!
     Death.   —And tragic; yet a fact.
              So make it snappy, Mister Santa Claus!
                    (*Exit. From the opposite direction enter Mob, furious: a little
                    girl follows*)

facing the furious Mob, Santa Claus at first denies that he's a
Scientist and asserts that wheelmines don't exist—but all in
vain.

     Voices. We say you're Science!   Down with Science!
Santa Claus.   —Wait!
              Ladies and gentlemen: if you all have been
              deceived by some impostor—so have I.
              If you all have been tricked and ruined—so have I.
              And so has every man and woman, I say.
              I say it, and you feel it in your hearts:
              we are all of us no longer glad and whole,
              we have all of us sold our spirits into death,
              we are all of us the sick parts of a sick thing,
              we have all of us lost our living honesty,
              and so we are all of us not any more ourselves.
              —Who can tell truth from falsehood any more?
              I say it, and you feel it in your hearts:
              no man or woman on this big small earth.
              —How should our sages miss the mark of life,
              and our most skillful players lose the game?
              your hearts will tell you, as my heart has told me:
              because all know, and no one understands.

                    —O, we are all so very full of knowing
                    that we are empty: empty of understanding;
                    but, by that emptiness, I swear to you
                    (and if I lie, ladies and gentlemen,
                    hang me a little higher than the sky)
                    all men and every woman may be wrong;
                    but nobody who lives can fool a child.
                    —Now I'll abide by the verdict of that little girl
                    over there, with the yellow hair and the blue eyes.
                    I'll simply ask her who I am; and whoever
                    she says I am, I am: is that fair enough?
      Voices.   Okay! Sure! Why not? Fine! A swell idea!
                    The kid will tell him who he is, all right!
                    Everybody knows!
Santa Claus.   —Silence! (*To Child*) Don't be afraid:
                    who am I?
      Child.   You are Santa Claus.
      Voices.   . . . Santa Claus?
     Chorus.   Ha-ha-ha-ha—there ain't no Santa Claus!
Santa Claus.   Then, ladies and gentlemen, I don't exist.
                    And since I don't exist, I am not guilty.
                    And since I am not guilty, I am innocent.
                    —Goodbye! And, next time, look before you leap.

When next we see our unhero, he is wondering if the little girl,
who (despite his deathmask) identified him as Santa Claus,
could perhaps be his own lost child. Our villain now appears,
emanating cordiality; and (in return for the good advice which
saved his almost victim's life) asks a favor

      Death.   I've got a heavy date
                    with a swell jane up the street a little way,
                    but something tells me she prefers plump fellows.
                    Will you give me your fat and take my skeleton?
Santa Claus.   With all the pleasure in the world, old-timer;
                    and I'll throw in a wheelmine, just for luck!
      Death.   No wheelmines, thank you.

They undress and exchange costumes; then off goes Death as Santa Claus, and in comes Child. Although the real Santa Claus is now completely disguised as Death, she immediately recognizes him; and before she dances away, he understands not only that he is her father, but that she—like himself—is looking for somebody "very beautiful. And very sad" who has lost them both.

Scene five follows—

>   (*Enter Woman, weeping*)
> *Woman.* Knowledge has taken love out of the world
> and all the world is empty empty empty:
> men are not men any more in all the world
> for a man who cannot love is not a man,
> and only a woman in love can be a woman;
> and, from their love alone, joy is born—joy!
> Knowledge has taken love out of the world
> and all the world is joyless joyless joyless.
> Come, death! for I have lost my joy and I
> have lost my love and I have lost myself.
>   (*Enter Santa Claus, as Death*)
> You have wanted me.   Now take me.
> *Santa Claus.*   Now and forever.
> *Woman.* How fortunate is dying, since I seem
> to hear his voice again.
> *Voices.* (*offstage*)   Dead! Dead!
> *Woman.* Could the world be emptier?
>   (*Tumult offstage.   She cringes*)
> *Santa Claus.*   Don't be afraid.
> *Woman.* O voice of him I loved more than my life,
> protect me from that deathless lifelessness—.
>   (*Enter Mob in procession, reeling and capering: the last
>   Mobsters carry a pole, from which dangles the capering and
>   reeling corpse of Death disguised as Santa Claus*)
> *Chorus.* Dead. Dead. Dead. Dead. Dead.
> *Voices.* Hooray! Dead; yes, dead: dead.   Hooray!
> Science is dead!   Dead.   Science is dead!
> *Voice.* He'll never sell another wheelmine—never!

Voices.	Dead! Hooray! Dead! Hooray! Dead!
Voice.	The filthy lousy stinking son of a bitch.
Chorus.	Hooray hooray hooray hooray hooray!
A Voice.	He fooled us once, and once was once too much!
Another.	He never fooled us, pal: it was the kid.
	(*Woman starts*)
Another.	Yeah, but the second time—boy, was that good!
Another.	I'll say it was!
Another.	Did you see the look she gave him?
Another.	Did you hear her say "*that* isn't Santa Claus"?
	(*Woman turns: sees the dangling effigy—recoils from the real Santa Claus*)
Chorus.	Ha-ha-ha-ha—there ain't no Santa Claus!
	(*Exit Mob, reeling and capering, booing whistling screeching*)
Woman.	Yes, the world could be emptier.
Santa Claus.	Now and—
Woman.	Never.
	I had remembered love—but who am I?
	Thanks, Death, for making love remember me.
	(*Enter dancing Child: sees Woman, and rushes to her arms*)
Woman.	Joy—yes! My (yes; O, yes) my life my love
	my soul myself . . . —Not yours, Death!
Santa Claus.	(*unmasking*) No.
Woman.	(*kneeling to Santa Claus*) Ours.

So ends the last lesson of a nondivisible ignoramus: a double lesson—outwardly and inwardly affirming that, whereas a world rises to fall, a spirit descends to ascend. Now our ignoramus faces the nonanswerable question "who, as a writer, am I?" with which his nonlecturing career began; and finds himself deluged by multitudinous answers. What would these multitudinous answers say if they could speak as a single answer? Possibly or impossibly this—

I am someone who proudly and humbly affirms that love is the mystery-of-mysteries, and that nothing measurable matters "a very good God damn": that "an artist, a man, a failure" is no mere whenfully accreting mechanism, but a givingly eternal complexity—neither some soulless and heartless ultrapredatory infra-animal nor any un-understandingly knowing and believing and thinking automation, but a naturally and miraculously whole human being—a feelingly illimitable individual; whose only happiness is to transcend himself, whose every agony is to grow.

Ecstasy and anguish, being and becoming; the immortality of the creative imagination and the indomitability of the human spirit—these are the subjects of my final poetry reading: which (I devoutly hope) may not wrong a most marvellous ode by Keats, and the magnificent closing stanzas of Shelley's Prometheus Unbound.

Thou still unravish'd bride of quietness,
    Thou foster-child of Silence and slow Time,
Sylvan historian, who canst thus express
    A flowery tale more sweetly than our rhyme:
What leaf-fringed legend haunts about thy shape
    Of deities or mortals, or of both,
        In Tempe or the dales of Arcady?
    What men or gods are these? What maidens loth?
What mad pursuit? What struggle to escape?
        What pipes and timbrels? What wild ecstasy?

Heard melodies are sweet, but those unheard
    Are sweeter; therefore, ye soft pipes, play on;
Not to the sensual ear, but, more endear'd,
    Pipe to the spirit ditties of no tone:
Fair youth, beneath the trees, thou canst not leave
    Thy song, nor ever can those trees be bare;
        Bold Lover, never, never canst thou kiss,
Though winning near the goal—yet, do not grieve;
        She cannot fade, though thou hast not thy bliss,
    For ever wilt thou love, and she be fair!

Ah, happy, happy boughs! that cannot shed
    Your leaves, nor ever bid the Spring adieu;
And, happy melodist, unwearièd,
    For ever piping songs for ever new;
More happy love! more happy, happy love!
    For ever warm and still to be enjoy'd,
        For ever panting and for ever young;
All breathing human passion far above,
    That leaves a heart high-sorrowful and cloy'd,
        A burning forehead, and a parching tongue.

Who are these coming to the sacrifice?
    To what green altar, O mysterious priest,
Lead'st thou that heifer lowing at the skies,
    And all her silken flanks with garlands drest?
What little town by river or sea-shore,
    Or mountain-built with peaceful citadel,
        Is emptied of its folk, this pious morn?
And, little town, thy streets for evermore

Will silent be; and not a soul, to tell
    Why thou art desolate, can e'er return.

O Attic shape! fair attitude! with brede
    Of marble men and maidens overwrought,
With forest branches and the trodden weed;
    Thou, silent form! dost tease us out of thought
As doth eternity. Cold Pastoral!
    When old age shall this generation waste,
        Thou shalt remain, in midst of other woe
    Than ours, a friend to man, to whom thou say'st,
'Beauty is truth, truth beauty,—that is all
        Ye know on earth, and all ye need to know.'

This is the day, which down the void abysm
At the Earth-born's spell yawns for Heaven's despotism.
    And Conquest is dragged captive through the deep:
Love, from its awful throne of patient power
In the wise heart, from the last giddy hour
    Of dread endurance, from the slippery, steep,
And narrow verge of crag-like agony, springs
And folds over the world its healing wings.

Gentleness, Virtue, Wisdom, and Endurance,
These are the seals of that most firm assurance
    Which bars the pit over Destruction's strength;
And if, with infirm hand, Eternity,
Mother of many acts and hours, should free
    The serpent that would clasp her with his length;
These are the spells by which to reassume
An empire o'er the disentangled doom.

To suffer woes which Hope thinks infinite;
To forgive wrongs darker than death or night;
    To defy Power, which seems omnipotent;
To love, and bear; to hope till Hope creates
From its own wreck the thing it contemplates;
    Neither to change, nor falter, nor repent;
This, like thy glory, Titan, is to be
Good, great and joyous, beautiful and free;
This is alone Life, Joy, Empire, and Victory.

LIST OF READINGS